PUBLIC SPEAKING PRINCIPLES

The Success Guide for Beginners to Efficient
Communication and Presentation Skills:

How to Rapidly Lose Fear and Excite Your
Audience as a Confident Speaker Without Anxiety

Gerard Shaw

FREE GIFT

This book includes a bonus booklet. Download may be for a limited time only. All information on how you can secure your gift right now can be found at the end of this book.

TABLE OF CONTENTS

INTRODUCTION..1

CHAPTER ONE 5

Modern Predators Can't Eat You 5

The Psychology of Fear 6

Acknowledging and Accepting Fear.......................... 10

Facing Down Your Fear... 12

Most of Our Fears Are Absurd 14

The NBA Star Turned Interview Comedian - Profile - Klay Thompson
.... 15

CHAPTER TWO 17

Your Audience Expects a Fearless Speaker 17

The Effects of Fear... 19

To Fully Express Yourself, Be Fearless 23

From Fired to Hired - Profile - Oprah Winfrey 25

CHAPTER THREE 27

Bravery in Modern Jungles..................................... 27

Practical Steps to Get Rid of Fear and Stage Fright 27

The Celebrity Who Fumbled, Only to Rise Again - Profile - Steve
Harvey.. 40

CHAPTER FOUR 43

Building Communication Skills................................. 43

Communication is About Connection.......................... 43

How to Adapt to an Audience.................................. 44

Verbal Communication 48

Non-Verbal Communication 52

Communication! Who Is It Good For? 57

The Singer Who Rose Above Her Fear with A Little Help - Profile - Adele 58

CHAPTER FIVE **61**

Crafting Amazing Speeches **61**

Pillars of a Speech 61

The Ultimate Beginning 66

Your Speech Outline 69

The Business Mogul Who Overcame His Fear - Profile - Warren Buffett 76

CHAPTER SIX **79**

Designing a Stellar Presentation **79**

Tools to Use 79

Building Your Slideshow 81

How A Golf Great Overcame His Stutter - Profile - Tiger Woods 90

CHAPTER SEVEN **91**

Successfully Attract Your Audience **91**

Lead the Way 92

Be Authentic 94

Finding Your Authentic Voice 96

Practicing Authenticity 97

Magnetism Comes from Within 101

The Actor Who Stepped Up Despite His Fears - Profile - Harrison Ford 102

CHAPTER EIGHT **105**

Avoiding Self-Sabotages **105**

About the Audience 105

About the Presentation... 111

Let Go of Mistakes.. 115

Overcoming Fear - Profile - You...................................... 116

FINAL WORDS **119**

REFERENCES...**121**

YOUR FREE GIFT IS HERE! **127**

INTRODUCTION

No one is born a naturally gifted public speaker. I wish I could say that I was phenomenal the first time I spoke in front of an audience, but that would be a lie. It took several failures for me to learn how to master public speaking. It's only now, after more than a decade of practicing and teaching public speaking, that I've come to have answers for those who want to take on their own public speaking career. Questions always range in topics, but most of them is about dealing with the fear that comes with public speaking. I realized that there are so many people starting out where I did, and so many of them want to learn how to overcome their fears before they step out onto the stage.

I want you to learn from what I've gone through before you begin your own journey. The concepts in this book are the ones I've applied in my own career, and they've allowed me and those I've mentored, success in their own public speaking goals. I know there'll be a time when you would probably run into the same moments I did earlier in my career. And where I failed miserably, I *know* you'll prosper.

In this book, I'll go over empowering solutions, along with detailed guidelines on how you can overcome your crippling fears. You'll gain the knowledge to help you develop and transform yourself into a confident and inspiring speaker. These are practical strategies for crafting winning speeches and properly articulating your core message.

1

I know these strategies will work for you because they've worked for me over my lengthy and in the beginning, sometimes difficult career.

You picked up this book, and that means there's a fire inside you that's pushing you forward and wanting you to become the presenter that leaves your audience in awe. Seeing that you have an interest in public speaking, there's an excellent chance that you're already engaged in giving speeches and presentations, maybe for professional, academic, civic, or social reasons. Whatever your reasons, I can only imagine the weight placed on you when you speak. Perhaps you hope these speaking engagements will lead to a fresh career path or a promotion. Regardless of the reasons, it's clear that you want to enhance your skills.

When I was younger, the thought of speaking in front of others made me cringe with fear. Having to stand in front of a class and introduce myself was enough to put me on edge. I had to forge a long and tedious path to become the successful public speaker I am now. I don't want you to have to tread that long, tedious path that I suffered through. Throughout my arduous journey, I've learned these concepts I'm about to share to you. It was only after my success using this knowledge that I began offering these secrets to my clients. I've seen incredible changes in many public speakers. Once they adopted the techniques, strategies, and methods in this book, novice speakers always returned with an overwhelming amount of appreciation for the confidence I helped them learn and the ways their public speaking career improved. Because of my coaching, I've seen people go from not even being able to step onto a stage, to wowing a crowd of hundreds while talking about what they love most.

You, too, can become a successful public speaker, overcome your fears, and forge your own path to success. The journey begins here.

- We will go over fear and the many ways it can cripple your ability to captivate an audience.

- You'll learn how to defeat your anxiety by using proven science-backed techniques.

- You'll learn to use techniques on how to build a speech, find your message, and deliver it with confidence!

All the concepts in this book have come from years of experience in training with world-class speakers, perfecting them over the years. You can now use them to build your own public speaking career. You'll be receiving all of this now!

If your earlier experience made you consider giving up on public speaking, by choosing this book you've proven that giving up isn't the solution. You probably have wasted enough time giving into your negative feedback loops. Beginning now, you no longer need to give those loops the power they *don't* deserve. Once you start acting on this book's sure-fire strategies, you'll notice the changes in yourself. You'll see just how your life can change now that you've taken the first step forward.

This book comes with a FREE booklet on masterminding a winning routine to improve calmness and your level of confidence daily. Head to the bottom of this book for instructions on how you can secure your copy today.

CHAPTER ONE

Modern Predators Can't Eat You

Let's face it - fear is essential for our biological self-preservation. Our ancestors needed fear to survive. It was a necessary sensation that played an enormous part in our past. In fact, you and I probably wouldn't be here today had our ancestors fearlessly chosen to stand around and get eaten by saber-toothed tigers instead of running away. So, fear has a purpose and an important one at that! That being said - it doesn't have the same function in our current society. The things we fear now just don't hold the same meaning as predatory felines did in the past. We live very comfortable lives and most of our present-day fears are mental phantoms we allow to threaten our present-day bliss.

Fear shouldn't determine our mindset and we should endure anxious moments. We can't ignore fear, per se, just let it run its course. Among the many emotions we harbor, fear is the succubus - it invades our subconscious, muttering to itself about the end of the world and stealing our confidence. It's paranoid and overpowers every other emotion while it's present. It constantly searches for danger, even when we're no longer running away from predators. Those types of adrenaline-pumping terrors stem from our ancestry - and that kind of fear is an outdated emotion. Our subconscious has no clue that, most of the time, we're *not* in mortal danger, and just giving a speech before strangers. This is how fear holds you back - it's always trying to get the upper hand. Fear stymies growth and like a demon, it enjoys keeping you in a bubble of suspicion.

So, send fear to the back of your mind and let it come out when you need it - not when you're about to take on public speaking. Fear doesn't belong there. *You* belong there, standing next to your confidence and pride. Leave fear behind the curtains muttering to itself about all the things that won't come to be. And just be there and do what you came for.

The Psychology of Fear

Primitive, irrational fear comes from the beginning of evolution. But, now, look around you. Let's face it - unless you're in the middle of a dangerous situation with this book on your tablet or in paper form, somehow being able to read - you understand that fear is an antiquated emotion. There's no doubt that it keeps us alive and safe, but it could be a hindrance to our everyday lives if we let it.

So, what is the *psychology* behind fear? Naturally, it's all in the mind, like a weed in a garden patch. Once planted in your thoughts, fear grows at the expense of your confidence. Real or psychological fear triggers a chemical reaction in every part of your body. Once your thoughts perceive a threat, your body goes into protective mode. That's when the physical reactions hit - sweating, shaking, and an increased heart rate. Everyone recognizes these warning signs and has felt it show up and expand. When anxiety hits, sometimes your stomach churns and an impending feeling of dread fills your entire body. Psychologists call this primal response the *flight or fight conflict;* in public speaking the emotion doesn't care if you have an audience to impress or an important message to communicate.

Trauma can leave marks on people's psychologies. These traumas can stem from past childhood experiences, but they can sometimes be from recent stage fright experiences that left an emotional imprint. Public speaking is a traumatic occasion for most people. Maybe you're one of those who had an unpleasant situation in the past where you misspoke words or fumbled on stage. Let me tell you this now: you're not alone. Many people have done those same things. Don't consider it as an emotional scar - consider it a stepping stone making up a learning curve. Keep in mind that there are more people out there who've made a mistake during a presentation than people who've given perfect presentations. That's a fact!

Fear takes place in memories, and if you let those overwhelm your current situation, you will run into the same issues repeatedly. It becomes a mental negative feedback loop, which rewires your brain to seek a familiar, and therefore comfortable failure. Irrational fear will inhibit your way of living should you give into it too often.

I know firsthand what kind of toll bad memories can take on future endeavors. Once, when I was speaking in front of a group, I made a joke that didn't land well. When outlining my presentation, I remember being proud of myself for coming up with this witticism. I was in the middle of my presentation and, well; the joke came up right on cue. My

7

audience was in a boardroom, and I had everyone's attention on me. I popped the joke, smiled, and waited for their response. Complete and utter silence follows. No one laughed. Not even a snicker. Now, silence can be a good thing in a presentation, but when humor fails, even veteran public speakers feel the tension.

So what did I do? I could have beaten myself up over the failed presentation for weeks, if not months, and I wanted to. I still remember how it left me feeling like I would be sick right there at the head of that table. I stammered. My face turned red. I could feel my heart racing. Did that bad joke haunt me for a while? Yeah. I'd be lying if I said it didn't. But I didn't let it stop me.

It took some time before I could look at myself in the mirror and figure out why I was so upset with myself. It was then that I knew I had to accept the situation. It was hard to say to myself that I'd screwed up; however, admitting I had a humor skill problem was the first step for improvement. Later, I asked myself what about this failure bothered me so much and why I was so nervous to give that presentation again. I confronted the issue the following week. I started that presentation so proud of myself, but my embarrassment and my reaction to the deadpanned crowd equaled a fright reaction. In reflection, I told myself that if I could have continued with my presentation as though nothing had happened, I wouldn't have felt so awful about it. *That* was my truth, and *that* was at the heart of my fear. It scared me to have that reaction next week. It embarrassed me about how my hands shook and the fact that I'd sweat through my light blue shirt throughout the presentation. I had to get to the core of my fear to prepare for the end of the presentation. So, once I knew that fear is just fear and could have no lasting consequences, I let go and made some changes. I wore black at the next presentation and eliminated the joke. The next time I presented, I stepped out in front of the crowd and had no issues. I found out I had nothing to worry about and walked away feeling a sense of pride.

That was me overcoming the situation by not giving in to my fear. Instead of giving in, I accepted it, figured out what it was, and made some necessary changes. Those feelings have come up again from time to time and those memories aren't gone, but I just don't give in to them. There are times you'll say things out of turn that causes *you* to sweat profusely. Just try not to pay that feeling of defeat too much mind. The people sitting there listening to your voice are genuinely interested in the information that you have to offer. They want you to succeed in filling their time meaningfully. Work with them, reject fear.

I know that this is a tough subject for many people. Emotional and physical insecurities manifest themselves in the same dry-mouthed, quivering knees responses. Knowing that you're not the only one feeling overwhelmed by public speaking can be reassuring. Confidence, like fear, is a complex emotion. When you understand that you choose how you react to fear, I know you'll learn how to look at the saber-toothed tiger in the eyes and refuse to let it dominate you. The first step is to acknowledge the tiger in the room.

Acknowledging and Accepting Fear

You now understand that fear of public speaking is psychological, and that you're not alone. So, let's get into how you can overcome it! Anyone can defeat their fear so long as they have the confidence to approach it and work on it. After all, people who fear public speaking often have psychologically negative feedback loops. In preparing to step in front of a crowd, the groundwork of overcoming fear starts with acceptance and acknowledgment, which are two practices that will improve your overall life satisfaction.

You must be aware of your emotions first and use them as a tool for self-improvement. Begin by keeping track of your emotions - maybe keep a journal for just a couple of days to find out how often emotions impact decision making. You must be honest with yourself about how and what you feel as they show up. It has to become a habit, so practice emotional awareness throughout the day.

When it comes to fear, you must remember to practice acceptance anytime that impending sense of doom sweeps over you. This is the opposite of ignoring it. For example, when you start to feel fear, allow it to happen, be aware of the sensations, objectively as possible, and watch how it unfolds at the moment, then conservatively consider your alternative responses after the fact. This latter part of the process will probably not happen during the event but is a positive personal feedback technique.

Avoiding negative emotions may seem like a survival strategy. There's nothing pleasant about feeling overwhelmed. We often just want the feeling to go away, and it's not the kind of thing you want sticking around, making you feel uncomfortable. And negative emotions - sadness, hopelessness, loneliness — can stress our bodies and reduce our otherwise positive energy. Unlike joy and public speaking successes, negative fear-causing emotions tend to stick around longer, even though we want them to pass quickly.

So, what's the first response we naturally have? We ignore it. It's an instinctual response that, if we simply disregard its presence, it will go away on its own. Unfortunately, it never really goes away on its own. These emotions linger until there's nothing for our bodies to do other than expel them, usually inconveniently. For example, when you're sad and you push it aside day after day, there'll come a time when you just burst out in tears. This is because you avoid the emotions. They end up having an adverse effect on your body and then erupt so you experience it at heightened levels after any given time. Suppression makes negative emotions worse. Think of your psychological body like a volcano - at some point, negative emotions are going to blow! When you sense this starting to happen, I want you to do something unfathomable - *accept it*. Yes, you read that right. Bring it on, hold it close like a long-lost relative. Hug the feeling like a planned response and then let it go.

For those of you who might be in denial, you might ask, "Why *should* you accept it?"

It's been scientifically proven that emotional avoidance is chaotic to your physical and mental wellbeing. Avoiding a situation because of fear becomes a trap because it's an easily accessible state of comfort that you grow accustomed to. When you ignore fear, you fake happiness by avoiding situations and people that trigger you. By avoiding the very things that brought you to fear in the past, you'll soon find yourself staying in and staying away from moments that could turn out to be fulfilling. Such rationalized comfort is like the runner who turns to junk food after a stone bruise sets him down for a couple of days — getting overweight is easier than standing up and risking an encounter with a stray rock. You'll become more fearful of the memory of the stone bruise than the actual pain, and the junk food will seem more comfortable than you can bear to give up. All because you avoid your fear.

Then there's the old, awful friend that we've all dealt with at one point or another - anxiety. When you're avoiding your fears, there's a raw sense of anticipation that comes along with it. You dread having to deal with it. Anxiety breeds itself. In fact, no! Anxiety feeds on itself. The best way to deal with fear is to accept it, including the physical and mental signs that accompany it. When fear gets magnified into a big, awful monster that you avoid, the Chihuahua becomes harder to face. No one wants to experience monsters, but just protect your ankles and there's no reason to let a tiny canine intimidate you. Move forward.

Facing Down Your Fear

You can't avoid fear. Accepting it and letting it go is the first step to wowing your audience. Once you've done that, there's only one thing left to do - face the fear and do it, anyway. It's not a secret that public speaking can be daunting. In fact, surveys have shown that public speaking ranked higher than death when it comes to our worst fears. Think about that. *Death*. Most people would rather die than speak in front of a crowd. This might come as a shock, or maybe you can relate to that feeling of dread. Regardless, if you've picked up this book, it means that you're ready to take it on full-force.

Here's the wonderful news! Facing your fear will calm your mind. Psychologists know that their phobic patients must face their fears to be cured. The same ideas help public speakers. Studies have proved that after you've faced a fear, you'll be overcome with an adrenaline-induced sense of well-being that sweeps throughout the body. Intense nervousness disappears, and, in the aftermath of euphoric success, you'll feel a sense of calm as cortisol hormone levels drop. This is why so many people take risks for a living - it's a natural high.

When considering the risks of first responders or military professionals, public speaking seems pretty tame. But, since many people would rather risk death instead of speaking in public, you place yourself above fear and in hero status when you constantly put yourself in the way of your stage fright. You might think, *why would I need to do that? I'm not a risk-taker. I don't live off adrenaline*. Well, science says you need to poke your fears until they no longer control you.

If you face your fears repeatedly, your mind will no longer see it as a threat.

Mentally beat up that bad boy stage fright over and over. *It will no longer be a threat*. The entire chemistry of your brain will change with this new acceptance and you'll no longer have the intense physical and

13

emotional symptoms towards the thing you fear. During this process, you'll want to avoid the very thing you're terrified of, but this is all about not giving in. Confront stage fright in little steps, indulge the shiver of your anxiety but feel it pass; you'll be able to train your body to feel anticipation for the rush of defeating your fear so it will no longer control you.

Most of Our Fears Are Absurd

Sounds pretty rough, doesn't it? Well, it's not meant to make you think as though your fears aren't valid - that's not what I'm getting at. What this means is that not all your fears are based in reality. I would say the majority of them aren't. Falling from that building? Yeah, that's definitely something to be afraid of. But standing in front of that crowd? Not so much.

What goes through your mind when you become fearful? Worst-case scenarios! Now, these worst-case scenarios are just that - scenarios. They don't exist yet and you have full control of what will happen next. They show up imagined and, like some kind of movie, show you all the worst things that could happen. It then gets replayed over and over again. The issue here? These moments you're seeing are all created in your mind. There's a good chance that they will never come to fruition. If you continue believing that these scenarios are real, then you're giving in to the feeling of dread that comes along with them.

This can also be considered as another form of avoidance. You're avoiding the thing that gives you anxiety and making it an even bigger problem - subconsciously it gives you excuses to not end up actually stepping up and facing it.

So, I want you to go over all your fears when it comes to public speaking. I want you to see them, accept them and acknowledge them, and then let them go. If you need to say it out loud, say it! But I want you to tell yourself, "These situations do not exist, and none of them will happen." If you can start to convince yourself using these sentences that you are safe, and that everything is made up in your mind, you're one step closer to overcoming your negative thought patterns. Your mind will then see these imagined scenes for what they are - your self-defeating imagination.

You'll start to feel good when you begin confronting your fears. There's an interesting and powerful way to build confidence by doing things you never thought possible - this is why some people live their lives as risk-takers. I want you to feel that pride that comes with being able to control how you react to your fears, and I know it's only a matter of time!

The NBA Star Turned Interview Comedian - Profile - Klay Thompson

If you're not an avid fan of the NBA, you may not know who Klay Thompson is. He's a five-time NBA All-Star and a three-time NBA champion. You'd think it would be easy for him to report on the sport he loves most, especially when discussing it in interviews. Unfortunately, Klay has had several instances of messing up while in front of the camera. These have made him a favorite among fans, but for all the wrong reasons.

One of the most notorious was when he gave a now-infamous interview after a winning game. Not only did Klay get tongue-tied, but he barely made sense. It went viral over Twitter and had many people laughing - pretty much at his expense.

So, what did Klay do? He didn't stop! He kept giving interviews, no matter what the occasion. He even showed up on local news segments to hone his interviewing skills. As a competitor, he knew that he had to practice to get better. Want to know the best part? He started incorporating humor. He eventually became a sort of comedian and soon became the funny man of NBA interviews.

He never let that moment, or a few of the others where he'd been embarrassed, bring him down. He overcame the Internet and journalists alike. You can now find compilations of his interviews where he's unabashedly himself and doesn't care about what people have to say about him.

CHAPTER TWO

Your Audience Expects a Fearless Speaker

I want you to think of someone you recognize as a fearless hero. Who are they? Why do you consider them *fearless*? I want you to consider what about them persuades you to believe that they have no fear. When I think of fearlessness, I think of people who've made a difference - Gandhi, Malala Yousafzai, or Martin Luther King Jr. These are all household heroes who have not only spoken to sympathetic and adversarial crowds but advanced our society's moral consciousness. Did they speak fearlessly? Absolutely. Do I expect you, as an emerging public speaker, to start a revolution? Maybe, in a sense, yes! I want you to revolutionize *your* life and give speeches and presentations about your passions. You and I want your voice to be heard because you have something to say. There's no doubt that whatever you're passionate about, there's an entire group of people who are passionate about the very same thing.

I know you'll be able to carry a room, while also becoming the best version of yourself. I want you to excel as I know you can - even in a stressful situation. You can forge your way ahead, becoming fearless despite the obstacles that you'll face along the way. This is all about building the confidence to be yourself and not look back on your fears.

It's always easy to think of fear as though it's an emotion *that's just there*. It often sits in the background like a child, kicking its legs when it wants attention. It may feel impossible to eliminate fear. However, fear is only as noteworthy as you allow it to be. You can still feel the emotions, acknowledge, and accept them, as mentioned previously, but it no longer needs to control you.

It probably sounds ridiculous. Who am I to talk to you about fearlessness? Well, I used to get so nervous before stepping out in front of a crowd I'd feel sick. It was like being filled with something else, not butterflies - my stomach would churn and I'd become dizzy. These are just some symptoms I'd have to deal with once I was about to step out in front of a crowd. It was difficult to look anyone in the eyes because I was so used to looking down. When I used to pass people in hallways, I'd be hunched over with my eyes to the floor. This was my natural state - and I had to change it. I didn't realize at the time, but I was stuck in a constant state of fear. I'd always think of the ways people would judge me. When I presented to an audience, though, I had no choice but to be noticed. How did I deal with that?

There was something I learned, though. After public speaking, I felt grateful for the fear I had before the event. There was always that sense of pride and relief that came afterward. It was bliss! But that bliss wouldn't have been possible if I didn't confront and overcome my anxiety and go forward with my passion. I want you to feel that too. Prepare to practice the steps in the next chapter by being able to recognize the effects fear has had on your day-to-day. By knowing the effects, you can then learn to tame your saber-toothed tiger and train it to roar on command.

The Effects of Fear

While we've all experienced the neurological impact of fear, recognizing the underlying issues causing fear can help us fight fear's symptoms. Even experienced public speakers deal with situational issues from time to time. Understanding the way our mind and body respond to fear will explain those bouts where you've had no control over your body or your thoughts. You must first know your enemy to defeat it.

Fear Paralyzes Thought

As a child, did you ever feel as though you were being watched by some malevolent ghost so you ended up freezing in place? Or have you awakened from a nightmare paralyzed in bed? It was like all your limbs were stuck in the same position and running wasn't even an option. What you experienced is what it means when people say, *"paralyzed with fear."*

Let me tell you this - it's common. So common that most people all over the world had it happen to them. It doesn't matter if you fear the dark or public speaking. This issue is one that has neurological origins from a *very* young age. Your ability to even hold memories in your mind wasn't developed yet. So, you ask, why haven't I outgrown this fear Well, it's a reflex. A naturally occurring reflex.

Fear Paralysis Reflex is a withdrawal reflex, and it starts as early as when we're in the womb. Yes, you were a fetus when this first appeared in the instinctually primitive part of your developing brain. Symptoms of FPR include difficulty breathing, feelings of being overwhelmed, isolation, withdrawal from touch, and many others. In the womb, you'd end up reacting to stressful situations by withdrawing and freezing, a kind of teamwork response with your mother's body, and both of you instinctively keeping you safe. The bad news? The learned responses to stress can stay on later in life, continuing the reflexive freezing even when no real threat exists.

Remember, public speaking is not a real threat. For you, the public speaker, the good news is that primitive functions can be trained like that wild predator in a cage. Your mind is the master of the beast.

Have you ever seen a movie where the lead character is about to go up on stage, finally makes it there, and then stands in complete shock while looking at the audience? Well, that's based on real life. It's a representation of FPR. It happens just as it does in the movies - your body reacts with FPR and you end up losing your thoughts just as your body shuts down physically clenching uncontrollably. Now that you know about FPR, know that, like anything, it can be overcome.

Fear Stifles Expression

Open body language combats FPR. It's all about showing that you have confidence, especially if you're nervous. Nothing portrays confidence quite as well as a strong physical presence. Humans subconsciously take in other people's body language every day. Our ongoing habits of reading body language are why sometimes remote communications - as in writing or texting - can result in misunderstandings. It's all because there's no body language to add to the meanings of the words we read. In public speaking, most people can correctly interpret a smile or embracing hand gestures or stepping forward as symbols of confidence. However, when fear shows up, you'll lose the ability to control your body's message, which can be a detriment to you while you're in the middle of a public speaking engagement.

It can take a lot of effort to maintain eye contact when you're nervous. When FPR adrenaline rushes through your body, all you want to do is run and hideaway. If you don't maintain eye contact it might look as though you're trying to avoid your audience. You should always remember that the audience invested their time and effort to gather to hear your message. If they feel you want to avoid them, they might see your message as not worth their attention, which is the opposite of what you want to portray.

Body language can be so meaningful and can encourage respect and engagement from your audience. So, be sure to encourage them with meaningful, spontaneous body movements and hand gestures, as these will direct everyone's eyes to where you want them to look, all while helping you express your presentation effectively. For example, persuasive speakers often build intensity with just a step back from the podium before fostering motivation by opening their arms wide.

Giving in to your nervousness will only cause your body to naturally start to close in on itself, as though you're trying to hide in plain sight.

21

It shows in your body language as dropped shoulders, a lowered head, and crossed arms - which shows to your audience you're uncomfortable. They'll subconsciously translate what they see into doubts about your message. Your expression, whether through body language or facial gesture, can be the difference between a bad or a good presentation or speech. You can't avoid emitting non-verbal cues, so if fear stifles your ability to express and makes your body naturally close off, a distracted audience may not hear the significant words you prepared for them.

Fear Disrupts Connection

You want to connect to your audience. Let me fix that statement. You *need* to connect to your audience. I'm sure you know that, and I'm sure that you're looking for that fire that will help you light the audience aflame - all while using only your words. This is the connection that can only be made when you're feeling confident and present. The issue here is that fear will affect your ability to do this.

Not only is fear breaking down your entire body with the physical sensations, but your mind gets set to mute. So you might forget your words or lose your train of thought when you're nervous. Nothing really connects when fear takes the wheel. FPR is a factor, but so are the neurological sensors in your mind. When fear takes over, it becomes difficult for the audience to read cues, both verbal and non-verbal. You'll have a harder time reading your audience as well.

It doesn't matter if you're just talking to a small boardroom of co-workers or doing a TED talk, I'm sure that connecting with your audience is of utmost importance. Allowing fear to take the wheel when you're trying to navigate is asking for trouble.

Fear Affects Your Mental Health

Your mental health is incredibly important when it comes to public speaking. After all, you want to be in the best state to present. Being on high alert consistently will impact your health in negative ways and, in turn, disrupt your presentations. You can't expect to motivate a crowd if you're suffering from fear and anxiety just from being around them. It's not easy to dig yourself out of a mental health issue, but you should seek ways to better it.

Beyond just the visual aspect of what fear does to your body language, it can affect your presentation further than what meets the eye. When you're practicing for your speech, you often go over certain sentences and information repeatedly. Fear interrupts your memory by debilitating the ability to form long-term memories. This is one reason why you have difficulty remembering certain words, phrases, facts, or punchlines. Studies found that anxiety impairs memories, thereby affecting work and personal relationships - not inhibiting the power of public speaking.

To Fully Express Yourself, Be Fearless

Expressiveness isn't just about emphasizing words, statements, or punchlines, or behaving over the top. You've met expressive individuals; you know how they affect people – everyone in the room pays attention. They have something about them that brings people in because there's always something to respond to. Typically, they generate different vocal tones, increase pauses, and mesmerize with a multitude of gestures and facial expressions. Being expressive isn't just about divulging all your life stories to your audience, or how naturally engaging the topic might be. It's about the way you present yourself. I understand that there's a fear that you might come off as too emotional or unprofessional, but that's not always the case - especially if you're expressive in the right ways.

Expression, in the way I describe it here, is more about being articulate, that what you're saying is tied to your own emotions. People interpret this kind of sincerity as authentic; we get into authenticity in a later chapter. When you're expressive, your voice conveys meaning regarding your subject. You will always appear as more charismatic and passionate because your voice and body support your words.

There's no denying it - being expressive is one of the best ways to captivate your audience. By using fluid motions, mixed with the meaningful gestures and the inviting way you use your voice, you can engage an audience's attention throughout. Turning loose your fear lets you exude fearlessness, allows you to overcome stiffness, removes barriers between you and your audience, and lets you connect. When you're being yourself, you'll find that you feel a natural state on stage.

Of course, you already know that being yourself isn't always simple. One great way of sharing yourself can be to put yourself into the presentation - literally! Feel free to share stories from your own life, or tell everyone how you feel about the product or the situation at hand.

24

You'll notice once you start doing this, it can become a more relaxing process because it's like you're sharing with friends. Remember the audience wants you to fill their time with meaning; getting to know you may be the important connection they seek before they accept your message.

From Fired to Hired - Profile - Oprah Winfrey

Now I know what you must be thinking: *how could Oprah Winfrey fail?* Her name is world-renowned, and she's considered a one-woman success story. She owns an empire completely built on her name. Oprah Winfrey is an incredible talk show host who became an author, an Oscar-nominated actress, and a TV mogul who owns her own channel and produces TV shows seen all around the world. She is known for her incredible voice and being able to interview even the most difficult of people. So, how is it that this amazing woman ever failed?

Well, Oprah was young once and, before she was the woman she is now, she was fired from her job as a news reporter at WJZ-TV in Baltimore. Yes, that's right. They fired *Oprah Winfrey*. It was a tough time for the talk show host, who had only just started her career.

"It shook me to my very core," she reminisced years later.

Oprah was told she was "unfit for TV." If she'd listened to her previous boss, she would never have had the life she has built for herself. She overcame her fear and went back on television, anyway. She relocated and became the voice for a failing talk show called *People Are*

Talking. Oprah would go on to become the ambitious, successful woman we all know today.

CHAPTER THREE

Bravery in Modern Jungles

Now that you have an idea of what fear can do to you, let's get into how to gain confidence while public speaking! These are the core concepts that will help you build yourself up so that no amount of fear will take you down. I've seen clients implement these over the years and see success in all their speaking engagements. It takes a lot of practice and control, but there's no doubt in my mind that you can achieve those same results! You *can* overcome your stage fright and learn how to take control when you step onto that stage. It all starts with building yourself up first.

Practical Steps to Get Rid of Fear and Stage Fright

Fear and stage fright go hand in hand, as one can't exist without the other. Stage fright is defined as *nervousness before or during an appearance before an audience*. It's a debilitating feeling that happens not only in your mind but in your body. It appears and causes you to lose faith and confidence in yourself faster than any other emotion

Stage fright can be frustrating to have to deal with day after day. Especially if you want to succeed in certain areas. After all, stage fright can cause you to fail an assignment or lose out on a promotion. It's like its number one priority is to hold you back! You should never feel embarrassed if you suffer from it. As I mentioned previously, surveys have proved that most people suffer from it. Everyone experiences fear in one form or another – this just happens to be one of yours.

There's more to it than that, though. First, we must start with fear, as it tends to be the number one enemy to those having to face an audience. You need to begin by understanding where your fear stems from so that you don't experience stage fright again. Once you find the deterrent that speaks most to you, you can then begin working on how to ease it.

I want you to be able to implement these steps into your own life, as they'll set you up for success while trying to conquer your stage fright and anxiety. If you complete all these exercises, I know that you'll feel intrinsically better. You owe it to yourself to try them and find which ones work best for you.

Each of these will no doubt take some work. You must practice them constantly for them to make a long-term impact. You'll need to remind yourself when you're speaking in public, when you're at work, or even when you're out with friends. You also must make time for yourself as you practice each of these steps so that you can start to hone in on them.

1. Silence Your Inner Critic

When we hear a voice in the back of our mind, it's not always an intuitive voice pushing you forward. This, unfortunately, is the voice you hear when you've made a mistake, or feel as though you're about to embarrass yourself. Your inner critic often appears out of nowhere, even when you're just minding your own business. It keeps you up while you lie awake in bed trying to sleep. Your inner critic stops you from achieving your potential, and it keeps you in your comfort zone.

There's no doubt that there are times when we need to listen, like before cheating on that test or yelling at the person we love. These are instances where we need to take a moment to hear where we've lost ourselves. However, these situations are far and few between - your inner critic does more damage in your everyday life than it does good.

Throughout our lives, it becomes second nature to fight ourselves over our shortcomings. Even if there are no external critics, your inner child hears, *"You're not good enough, no one likes you or you're wasting your time."* Sabotaging thoughts like these do not reflect your true reality! We created these deceptions about ourselves, and they nag until we come to believe them.

I'm here to tell you to silence that voice. That voice emerging from your apprehension closet is not you. Your inner critic is doing you no good by traipsing around in your mind telling you terrible lies about yourself. That cranky critic only hinders you from growing. If you examine it, you'll remember that such negativism is often born of difficult childhood memories or unhappy encounters with negative people. Letting that negative vocal loop play will sabotage not only the moments before an important event but your future happiness because failure will get to be a habit.

One way you can silence your inner critic is by daily practicing self-affirmations. Instead of hitting auto replay on the negative loops in your past, record new scripts beginning with *I'm getting better at this every day*. By changing the monologue, you strangle negativity. Watch for the pity voice when it appears and alter it into a powerful voice that better suits your needs.

As mentioned previously, like fear, your inner critic must be acknowledged. Hear what it has to say and then make a conscious effort to let it go. If you relinquish emotions attached to that voice, you'll soon forget that it exists at all. Your inner critic will come up again, but when it does, you won't worry about it - strictly because it's not necessary anymore. You'll hear it and then release it without feeling a thing.

If you find that your inner voice is overwhelming, you can always write down what it says. Some people keep journals or use the notes app on their phones - you can decide what works for you. Write down what it says, even though it might be painful. Looking at your doubts written down, you might even believe them. Don't give in, though. Once you see those words written out, it'll expose their irrationality. Respond by writing next to it the truth. For example, if you write, "No one wants to hear me," you can then edit that script with, "I have something important to say and people enjoy listening to me."

Overcome negativity. Practice positivity. Reading positive affirmations you write down will start to form until you believe them. Let those optimistic words become the new voice in your head. Repeat them to yourself until they become law. This is one instance where some old adages - like *fake it till you make it* and *practice makes perfect* - really hold true.

2. Visualization

You may have never heard of visualization, but I'm sure you've practiced it before without even knowing. If you've ever imagined yourself walking onto a stage and accepting an award, or dreaming about driving a specific car, then you've implemented visualization into your life. This is a core concept that you can use to ease your anxiety before a big speech or presentation. Not only will it help you face obstacles, but it will help you imagine how to proceed with nerve-wracking situations because it'll feel like you've already accomplished them.

Why would you use visualization? Well, science backs it up! Studies have proven that when you're visualizing, the brain can't tell if what you're experiencing is real or not. Whenever you imagine a situation vividly, the chemistry in your brain will change to compliment what you're seeing. For example - if you're imagining winning a trophy, the muscles in your arms will start to fire as you imagine yourself raising the trophy because your mind thinks it's really happening.

As you now know, fear can often stem from the anxiety of imagining that something bad will happen before the situation becomes reality. Instead of allowing that situation, visualize yourself doing whatever you are set to do, such as a toast or a presentation. Your visualization will have you feel as though you've already succeeded.

Let's get into how you can practice visualizing right away. First off, the best way of visualization happens when you're alone in a space where you know you'll be relaxed. Choose an area of your house where silence is your only audience. For a truly relaxed approach to visualization, lie down in bed, or sit in a comfortable chair. Breathe deeply three times and close your eyes. See your speaking venue. Imagine the friendly faces you find in the audience and imagine the wealth of knowledge you prepared for this occasion.

Now, when you start imagining how you want the situation to go, focus on the small things so that the scene becomes more vivid. Imagine how warm the room is, what your hands are doing, how loud your voice is. It's these small details that will make it more realistic for you. Think warm, happy thoughts about your opportunity here. This is your performance. Really *feel* the emotions you know you'll have after giving an outstanding presentation. You can also give in and *feel* the excitement of capturing the audience with your speech. You know your message is worthwhile; now imagine other people agreeing.

Once you've finished your visualization, allow yourself to breathe slowly and come back to the room. Relax and feel those positive emotions flowing through you. That sensation inside your chest is confidence and pride. This is a good thing! Keep that feeling and bring it with you to your public speaking engagement.

As a novice speaker, practice visualization at least three times a week, if not more. Rehearsal is always a confidence booster. Practicing positive anticipation will also keep away those negative moments that

32

we tend to picture if we haven't retrained our emotions to be strongly supportive.

3. Be in the Moment

Being mindful is not mystical. I'm definitely not going to tell you to stand up on stage and chant in front of the audience in a lotus pose. This is about being in the moment and feeling as though you're in the right place, with the right people, your audience. Being in the moment is key to giving a great presentation.

Until you practice and master the technique, there's no doubt that, even if you've heard the phrase, you may find it hard to describe what *being in the moment* entails and why it's so important. It's something so many people talk about, but we all struggle doing. So, I can already hear you asking me, "What do you mean in the moment? I'm in the moment right now, idiot." Yeah, but no. You might think you're in the moment, but that's just it – you're *thinking*. If you focus so much on the little details, you miss the big picture. Being in the moment is more about seeing everything but filtering out any distractions interfering with your message.

I will describe it this way. Have you ever been in a flow? I'm not talking about a river where you're bobbing up and down. Flow is when you enjoy doing something so much that you lose yourself in the process and time flies by. When you're in a flow, you're in the moment. There's usually a sense of calm involved. It's all about taking a moment to relax your thoughts!

What's one of the first things that you wanted the presentation to be before you've even started? Over with. Yeah, that's probably not the first thing that came to your mind, but I know it shows up right before the presentation starts and your heart jumps off the starting blocks ahead of your words. I can remember back when I was younger and in school. There was always that dread when I knew it would be my turn to present in front of the class. My hands shook. My backbone turned to jelly. I watched the last presenter wrap up and dreaded standing up to walk forward. I wanted my speech finished, over and done within moments if not sooner. Then, my moment passed because I was never really there; I was too busy trying to skip to the finish anxiously to the end of the presentation.

You may have found yourself in a similar situation. Your dread denied you the pleasure of your preparation. Speakers just going through the presentation motions suck the life from the opportunity and what the audience sees and hears quickly becomes dull. If we're so eager to be quick on our speech, the audience knows and they want it over with too. So, the best way to keep yourself in the moment is to take a step back and assess what it is you're saying. You may be stuck with a speech topic you're not too excited about, but there must be something dynamic you can do with the message to make it come alive. Once you start making it interesting for yourself, you'll find that others want to listen even more.

Great speakers often pause before they launch their message. They are finding the moment to take a few deep breaths while the audience adjusts to the change. Inside themselves, those great speakers find a quiet mental space. Scanning the audience for benevolent listeners, they breathe in through the mouth and exhale past the nostrils, relax their shoulders and then calmly take charge of their opportunity. Practice this as many times as you need until you feel your heartbeat easing.

4. Fake It 'Till You Make It

Fake it till you make it. It's a sentence I'm sure you've heard before, but it can have a lasting impact on your confidence. Just like editing a written speech shapes the message into a tighter, more meaningful format, most often making your body act confident ensures that you're in a powerful position that can affect the outcome of your presentation.

Any superhero has a pose so perfect it becomes an icon in people's minds. Hours of mirror experiments must be part of that pose phenomenon, right? Consider this: in her now-famous TED talk, Amy Cuddy, a Harvard Business social psychologist, shared the effects of how powerful poses can change body chemistry. She developed a study where her subjects did various stances. In one group, subjects struck power stances where they placed their hands on their hips and raised their heads high. In the adverse experiment, subjects practiced lowering their heads and allowing their shoulders to slump. Her study discovered that physiologically those who practiced power poses experienced heightened testosterone and lower cortisol, a hormone present during intrusive stress. Cuddy's experiments proved that positive behaviors created chemically enhanced confidence in her subjects. Confidence allowed her subjects to demonstrate dominance that leads to more confidence. All this confidence just from striking a superhero pose.

Based on Cuddy's proof, when you feel nervous before stepping out into that boardroom or onto that stage, practice a powerful pose. Stand tall with your head held high, place your hands on your hips, and open up your chest. You can also choose to lift your hands high as though you've just won a race. These are poses that cause the testosterone in the body to rise, which sends a signal to your brain that you're feeling confident. It's a naturally occurring phenomenon that happens with the body and will help you ease some of the interfering natural tension.

While you're faking power, allow yourself to feel as though you've already become a successful public speaker. Tell yourself a manta day after day that helps you feel this way. For example, say sincerely, "Everyone applauds me when I walk onstage." It's a simple visualization, but it's just one way to feel as though you've already made your mark in the public speaking world. After a time, you'll gain the confidence to stand out there and feel as though you do have something important to say to the audience, and you won't fear their gazes. Become that person even if you don't feel like it at first. In just a few moments you'll find that your body aligns with that stance and you'll unconsciously become the very person you're pretending to be. With practice, you can be that person, and it's only a matter of moments until you are.

5. Don't be Afraid to Learn

We already know that you're not born a master at public speaking. Sure, you might have been outgoing as a child - this doesn't mean you were meant to move crowds. It typically means you were cute and liked to bust a move at weddings. No one wakes up at the age of three and decides to be a master public speaker. A veterinarian, sure. A firefighter? Yeah, that sounds about right. The kind of person that can stand in front of a crowd and wow them with voice, intellect, and a powerful vocabulary? Not really. This is the beautiful thing about public speaking, though - you can learn as you go. It's meant to be a learned skill that evolves upward the more you practice.

Public speaking is an ancient art, but learning to be effective now involves learning new, rapidly changing strategies. No matter the circumstance, you should always be learning. With society changing and adapting, be certain you are meeting the world on its terms. Even when you think you're done learning a new skill, there's always something new that comes around. In public speaking, there's an immense amount of diversity with the technology involved with presentations. Continuously honing your skills allows you to have success in your future endeavors. You should always learn new advantages – that's the only way to become a professional.

Professionals adapt and never let fear step in. Often, when we're faced with something new and challenging, it's easy to procrastinate. It's hard to stand up, raise your hand, and say, "Yeah. I want to make mistakes!" The issue, too, is that you will make mistakes, exposing your imperfections but making you try harder. If you're already trying as hard as you can, adaptations can certainly push you to the brink of your comfort zone, and that's why fear can reappear – the FRP monster knows that you're nervous. You must push past it and evolve your skills anyway.

Practice public speaking more so the better you'll become. Remember, there's no real threat to getting nervous. There are no real tigers. Give yourself some space to feel those nerves, and accept them, tame them. You will learn to master public speaking and that's all part of the fun! Learning new skills fortifies our mental health and sense of well-being. So have fun with it. Practice until your voice hurts. Do those powerful poses. Envision yourself speaking to hundreds of people and inspiring a crowd. If you do all these things, you'll discover that you were already that person that you were looking to become - you just need to hone those skills. It's as Bruce Lee once said, "Knowing is not enough. We must apply. Willing is not enough. We must do."

6. Believe in Yourself

It's a phrase we've all heard - *believe in yourself.* Ever since you were little, people have said it. It's on posters, in movies, and books. It's an overused phrase that, at this point, doesn't seem to hold much meaning anymore except to those people, professionals, who practice the exercise. Unlike the athlete whose body parts can wear out, the constant practice of self-belief only gets stronger. Find a believer at peace with who he or she is and watch the audience respond to that confidence. You can be the same kind of dynamic speaker.

7. Comparison Depletes Confidence

Let's say, hypothetically, you have a speaking engagement at a convention. You, with your message and a particular set of speaking skills, may have to follow a dynamic public speaking superhero. If the crowd responses told you they loved the last guy, you may start to beat yourself up before you get to the podium, fearing you won't be as good. Remember, it's too late to compare your notes and your visual aids to his, and so what if his punchlines always got laughs? Self-doubt happens when we compare ourselves to others. Never trick yourself into believing that someone is better than you because *you* think they are. They might be just a little more skilled, and you use that; You're unique, and your presentation is deserving of being heard. Your voice matters. No one can take that away from you, except you. Set aside comparing yourself, focus on your own work, and stand up there knowing that you have something new to say.

8. Attitude of Gratitude

When you begin to practice gratitude in your life, you'll begin to notice subtle changes in your day-to-day attitude. It starts small, but gradually grows the more you practice. You're probably wondering what being grateful has to do with your ability to believe in yourself. I know that they seem like separate subjects, but they're really not. Being able to show gratitude for the small things in your life will begin to lift you from a place of self-pity. Not only will it help you develop a positive attitude, but you'll discover that there's more to you than just the negative aspects. This is crucial to building joy in your life.

You can choose to write down several various things you're grateful for in the morning and get started with your day. You can also choose to do it right before your next public speaking engagement. If you feel your nerves getting the best of you, you can always choose to start a mental list of things you're grateful for. These can range from the venue that you've booked, your job, or even the outfit you're wearing. You'll find that not only will it help you relax, but you'll go into it believing that you deserve to be there – all because you were grateful.

The Celebrity Who Fumbled, Only to Rise Again - Profile - Steve Harvey

He's charming, funny, and the host of his TV talk show. He's a household name who has authored books and spoken to crowds for most of his career. However, there was one mistake made one evening that was heard all around the world. When Steve Harvey took on the role to host Miss Universe in 2015, he wasn't expecting to make a catastrophic mistake. When announcing the Miss Universe winner, he accidentally announced the wrong contestant's name. Impromptu and on live television, Harvey owned up to his mistake, apologized, and announced the corrected winner's name, recanting the previous 15 seconds of mistake before an international audience.

The next few weeks would be the hardest of Steve Harvey's career. Tabloids the world over screamed Harvey's mistake in large black letters. In the weeks following, Harvey found himself the laughing stock of news channels and comedians, his gaff resurrected repeatedly on the cover of magazines for the whole world to see. Even his innocent family wasn't spared, receiving death threats because of Harvey's unintentional mistake on stage. Of course, that put Harvey in a position he'd never felt before.

Owning up to his part in the mistaken announcement, Harvey took steps the very year to capitalize on his mistake and thereby caused another uproar. Instead of fading away into humiliation, Harvey hosted the Miss Universe pageant the very next year and made jokes about his difficult situation. He took all of his fear, bottled it, set it aside 12 months, and stepped back out onto the stage. Courageously Harvey told jokes on himself throughout a flawless pageant. One of the jokes was a skit with the former Miss Universe delivering a pair of reading glasses to the stage before his big announcement. Good humor, grade under fire, and professional strength let Harvey manage to put the whole spectacle behind him, and all because he stepped back out onto that very stage that he'd first made his big, nearly career sinking mistake.

CHAPTER FOUR

Building Communication Skills

You can't become a renowned public speaker without being able to communicate with your audience. Knowing how to adapt, connect and thrill your audience will lead you to be the best presenter you can be.

Communication is About Connection

I want you to think of a close friend of yours. What is it that makes you friends? Is it the things you do together? Maybe you both like the same bands? Let me answer this for you, as I'm sure you're already thinking the same thing - heck, no! What makes us care about people, things, and situations is *not* the thing itself, but often the connection we have to it. Yes, you might hear a certain song and enjoy it. Often, though, it's about feeling connected to that song at the moment. Something about that song moves you. That's what makes a brilliant public speaker. If you can connect to your audience and I mean, really *connect* with them, then you're looking at presenting successfully.

But how can you connect to complete strangers? It's not like you're going to go out for a drink with them after your meeting and talk about that TV show that you both happen to watch. No, that would be a definite connection but it wouldn't be because of your presentation. You want to be able to connect with them from the stage - which is even harder to do.

How to Adapt to an Audience

Okay. You've had those days when you want to crawl into a hole because of something you said or did. This could be saying a bad joke in front of a group of friends or giving a customer the wrong amount of change. Regardless, guess what? We've all been there! Especially with bad presentations. Whether it was in your childhood, or even now, it's likely you've been forced to sit through a presentation that makes you want to fall asleep or jump out of your seat and run for the door from boredom. There are a few reasons why those other presentations were so bad. They could have been too over-the-top on trying to sell you something; maybe the person giving the presentation had no charisma, or maybe the presentation was half an hour longer than it should be. It doesn't really matter. You sat there wishing you had your time back.

As public speakers, we certainly want to avoid punishing our audience as we were once punished. Fortunately, those punishing presentations are rare; most often, when they happen, the real cause is because the speaker failed to adapt the presentation to the audience. Speaking skills can be a real reason for memorable bad jobs. For instance, when you were younger maybe one of your classmates mumbled every other word, talking way longer than they needed, or didn't make the topic interesting by throwing in some passion and knowledge. What's the defining feature here? Well, it's the lack of entertainment for a younger crowd. A group of young students won't want to sit still for that long listening to someone without a proper voice! Of course, it was awful.

But, you, the seeker of oratorical skills, aren't that mumbling, bumbling, scared presenter. Still, keep this in mind: *Public speaking isn't about you. It's about the audience.* Now, repeat that rule a few times until it sticks - because it's vital to a great speech or presentation.

Meet Them Before

For the sake of the audience, and the eventual respect they give your message, do these adaptations; by the way, these professional connection skills work in everyday life and relationships as well. First, know who your audience is. No matter what type of public speaking you're doing, you need to know as much as you can about your demographic. This means you want to know them. This is the only way your speech or presentation will meet their needs and keep them captivated. No one expects you to stalk social media profiles, just be a student of people. When possible, background research the group you're presenting to; find out why they associate with each other. If circumstances are more intimate and the opportunity exists, introduce yourself at the door. This way, if you're unsure of what kind of audience you have, eye contact and a few words of greeting can help gauge the audience's general backgrounds and ages as they step inside.

Speak Their Language

The way you speak should be guided by whom you're speaking to. For instance, the way you speak to your boss will be very different from the way you speak to friends at the pub. In public speaking, the

45

background of the audience can dictate the language, tone, and word choices. Retired professors will need to hear you be different from the way you'd speak to a group of high school construction trades students. If you can figure out your demographics, you'll find your voice while speaking to them. You can then manage your tone, what you say, and how you say it. This way you can fine-tune your presentation to perfection. It helps you define what kind of words you're going to use. If you're not sure about your demographic before you go into your presentation, make broad statements but set up a few key points to adapt. Part of this can be done using an audience engagement survey. Get the audience participating in your presentation by asking non-threatening rhetorical questions they can raise a hand toward indicating their preferences of answers. Asking audiences to participate in paper surveys after the show can collect data you can use to adapt to future presentations. The big idea is to get audience connections without being intrusive. The side benefit is that collecting information gets the audience thinking about what you're presenting.

Find Out More

Usually, you're scheduled to speak at a specific venue. If you're unsure about the area and the typical demographic, you can always ask the organizer about audiences that show up. You can find out what they typically respond to, and get to know the type of people that frequent the venue. If it's a professional meeting with another agency or a client, you can always ask the manager what you can expect. You can always familiarize yourself with them beforehand so that you're better prepared. The point is—never be afraid to ask. This can only help you in the long run.

Get to Know Them

You can't make a connection with some people without formally knowing them first. There are a multitude of ways that you can go about this. You can just get to know them after and during the presentation so that you can know what kind of demographic is interested in your topic. Feel free to ask questions to the audience, create a survey, or introduce yourself if some people are waiting for you afterward. It makes all the difference, and it helps you acclimate in front of them better. You can also choose an option that works best with your presentation and whichever one you feel more comfortable with. It also makes the presentation feel more personal for them because they now have a personal stake in your subject so they'll be more receptive while you're speaking.

They Want You to Succeed

The crowd may be seen as the enemy when it comes to public speaking, and it can feel overwhelming when stepping out onto the stage. I'm sure you remember the stereotypical advice that comes with the crowd—imagine them naked. Well, let's *not* actually do that. Yes, public speaking can be terrifying. It's like walking up to a guillotine. There's always the assumption that we're going to be judged the minute that we walk out with all those eyes on us. Any mistakes will be remembered forever. Fortunately, that's not always the case.

You'd be surprised to know that your audience isn't always against you. Some want to be entertained, while others are there to learn. They don't want you to mess up in front of them—it's the opposite. They want to see you succeed. This is the opposite of what we normally learn from movies and books. Usually, the main character is belittled in front of a crowd a la Stephen King's Carrie. Real-life doesn't happen that way, though.

I want you to think about when you were a part of that audience. When you see the speaker mess up, you don't automatically jeer them. This isn't stand-up comedy where you can heckle the comedian to make them notice you. No, this is on a completely different level. The typical reaction to someone losing their train of thought in front of a crowd is not to berate them. It's the opposite – you feel bad for them. You want them to just stumble through and continue from where they left off. There's a feeling that washes over the whole crowd when this happens.

So, to adapt to your audience, you always need to remember that they want to see you win. They're there to be entertained. They're not thinking of how you're going to fail in front of them and how great that will be. I'd go as far as to say they're supporting you. Don't go in assuming you're heading to a death sentence. It's anything but that. You're going out there to win.

Verbal Communication

What involves verbal communication? Well, it's essentially consisting of your words and voice. When using both with fluidity, you'll find that you're like a conductor orchestrating a symphony, and word choices and voice tone make up half the battle when winning over your audience. Physically, if your voice takes up fifty percent of your communication, that could very well be enough to hook listeners, even if your other fifty percent (body language) isn't up to par.

When I mention voice and words, I'm not talking about the gist of your presentation or speech. That is a completely different topic. When I cover the physical half of verbal communication, I'm talking about your tone, the speed of your words, and the loudness of your voice. Each of these is crucial to public speaking whether a microphone is available or not. For example, if your voice is too low and doesn't project well enough, there's a good chance that some people may not hear you. Also, poor articulation, pronunciation clarity, can leave audiences confused and wondering why they bothered trying to listen at all. Therefore, actual verbal skills matter - not only will these skills be inclusive of everyone, but a distinctive speaking voice can also keep everyone's attention.

Pausing

Pause. And go. Pause. And go. Just by reading those words, your mind automatically pauses and hangs on. When you're speaking to an audience, the same thing happens. You can pause for effect when you're speaking to keep your audience on the edge of their seats. There are a few different pauses you can use to get the best results. Most of these pauses can be used in anything - a presentation, a speech, or even just while in a meeting. However, be sure to use them minimally and keep the pauses short. An intentional pause for effect held too long becomes an awkward pause. The last thing you'd want. Make sure pauses remain shorter than 4-5 seconds long. Any longer and the audience's brains could move to new distractions. Be sure you know your motivation why you pause:

- *Reflective pause* - This is when you use a pause to get the audience to reflect on what you just said. To accomplish this, you ask the audience to reflect on the topic at hand. You can say something like, "Now, we'll take a minute to think about how this will affect you."

- *Dramatic pause* - this pause is used when you're looking to add effect to what you've been saying. Usually, this pause is used to get the audience to hold their breath, and tighten tensions right before a punchline or a dramatic declaration.

- *Topic pause* - this pause provides transitions between topics. Don't drag out this pause too long when you only want your audience to understand that you're shifting the focus from one area to another.

- *Visual pause* - are you about to bring up a new visual aide shortly after speaking on a different topic? No matter whether it's the number of sales accrued in graph form or a picture of something related to your core message, you can always pause in between visual displays. This allows your audience to take in the information before you start speaking about it right away.

Have you ever been to a theatre and just when the scary villain is about to pop out, everyone falls silent, waiting for the moment? That's what happens when you use pauses effectively. Be sure to incorporate them to establish tension in the room.

Slowing It Down

Your topic is important to you, no matter whether it's a professional topic or an informational topic. Emphasize your topic and lead your audience without them realizing, and all by slowing down the way you're speaking and by articulating your words. Slowing down also exercises power over your nerves and shows that you have authority on the subject at hand. Altering vocal pace is pleasant for listeners and gives them time to reflect on the topic at hand.

Never rush through your words at such a pace that the tone of your voice heightens with strain. Audiences interpret fast words with something unimportant, commercial, or trivial that can easily be skimmed over. You exemplify for your audience which information is most significant, which statements are most credible, and what parts of the presentation are most appreciable - all by slowing down.

Emphasis

You can get a whole new sentence just by emphasizing certain words. It helps to add variety and can clarify your core message to more people. See these examples:

- The *future* is in our hands.

- The future is in *our* hands.

51

So, emphasize your presentation's key topics. Emphasis will be particularly important in your concluding remarks; there you'll want to summarize, motivate, or make your audience think. You can get two very different results by changing your tone towards a particular word, so be sure to practice which one you're looking to focus on.

Tone

Voice tone conveys emotions so you want those emotions clearly understood. Like an actor, you must practice different pitches, timbres, and vocal force to match your message. For instance, if you want to convey sadness about something, you can lower your tone to a deeper pitch, add a quiver in your vocal cords, and execute a stage whisper. If you're looking to get everyone riled up by your subject, you can crescendo the tone of your voice while resonating from your chest and projecting to the back rows of the venue. Especially when speaking informatively, remember to keep your overall pitch pleasing to listen to. When practicing, modern technology lets most people record their voices so they hear how audiences perceive their speech strategies. You can do the same if you're unsure if you're hitting the right tone.

Non-Verbal Communication

Our subconscious automatically picks up on body language. In fact, there are also those who have been able to read body language for a living. That's because each person, no matter who they are, has body language that's subjective of how we're feeling and what we're doing. This is incredibly important, especially when you have people watching you. That's why you should always keep in mind that your body should be telling a story, alongside your words and the way you speak them.

It's all about being in control of your body. So even if you might be freaking out internally, you can make it so that your body is saying something completely different! There are small areas you can focus on to maximize the effects of your body language on your audience.

Hands

All right, let's get down to the obvious part - your hands. You want to speak with your hands. Studies have found that the most popular TED talk speakers used about 465 hand gestures, nearly double the amount of those who weren't nearly as popular. So, integrate those hands! You may find that those who speak with their hands can be a little distracting, which is understandable, as they're often right in front of you and speaking one on one. Here's the great part though - you want to keep people's eyes on you.

Not only do hand movements allow you to convey your message better, but hands can be a great way to attract your audience's attention to particular details they may not have noticed. For example, during a wedding speech, usually, the person conducting the toast keeps their glass in their hand, ready at any moment. This gives everyone in the room anticipation for when they will, in turn, raise their glasses to toast to the couple. This is a social example of where audiences understand body language and gestures.

When rehearsing your presentation, consciously incorporate enough hand movements to keep any audience's eyes towards the board for your presentation or toward your face when you want to express something important. Use your hand gestures to emphasize your words, and you'll find that public speaking will feel even more natural to you.

Eyes

Maintain eye contact is probably the most important advice given to anyone interested in mastering public speaking. Eye contact may also be the most difficult tactic for shy speakers to learn. Confidence emanates from direct eye contact, so new speakers should find friendly eyes in a quick audience scan and speak to those. The impact of establishing that one-on-one contact will spread across the adjacent listeners, keeping their attention. Also, your eyes, when used correctly, can bring in those of the audience who may not be paying attention back to your message. If you're staring at the floor the whole time, you'll find that your audience will quickly become bored.

Eyes communicate people's intentions, as eyes can sometimes be the most expressive part of our face. When we make eye contact, we automatically assume the person we're speaking to has confidence equal to our own; this holds true whether you participate as a speaker or listener. You should keep eye contact in mind, even if you're speaking to a large audience. Scan over them, and take in their expressions. Acknowledging them can be a great way to keep their attention.

As with much of our nonverbal communications, experienced speakers make eye contact subconsciously. Among our intimate communicators, we seldom plan our eye messages. Such as when you're angry with someone, you might squint your eyes at them. When you see someone upset like that, you don't even need to see their body expression - all you need is to see their eyes. Therefore, as the speaker, you want to maintain eye contact properly. Keep your eyes soft and open so the audience feels you are not judging them or are antagonistic toward them. Who needs a room full of antagonized listeners?

Posture

Look in the mirror and stand as you typically do. This is your average posture, and although it might be comfortable for you - it's not typically the posture you need to have while public speaking. When you're standing in front of a crowd it's best to use your *public speaking posture.*

Ideally, a good speaker leads with the chest raised so the back's straight. You want to stand with a slight lean toward the audience as though the people in the room are pulling at your heart. Demonstrating an open, accepting posture is to not be as stiff! You want to utilize your whole body to communicate with your audience, so practice your posture before you step out on stage. This posture often leads with authority and confidence - perfect for public speaking.

Energy

Honing in on an energetic presence doesn't mean that you have to do backflips before your presentation or entertain the crowd like a popstar. No, this simply means that you'll want to keep a light tone to your voice and move around. If you move during your presentation, even a little bit, you'll catch the eyes of anyone who may not have been paying attention.

When you're more energetic, people will naturally see you as being warm and approachable making their connection to you, and your message, easier. Having great energy is like looking at the crowd and yelling, "LISTEN TO ME!" without actually yelling it aloud.

There are some proven ways you can get yourself energized before a presentation.

Some people, like the public speaker great Tony Robbins, exercise before they head out on stage. I'm not telling you to run a marathon, but you could always do some jumping jacks before the presentation to get your heart racing - in a different way than nerves will give you. Robbins prefers to jump on a jogger's trampoline while inhaling and exhaling quickly to get his blood rushing. Even doing a few push-ups will give you a little adrenaline kick and take your mind off the crowd before you start.

If you're having trouble keeping up energy during your presentation, re-engage the audience by telling a story that matters to you. Anything anecdote that evokes emotion in you will help you bring up the drama in the room and add depth to your voice. Walking back and forth in front of the audience from time to time, which will bring eyes to focus on you again.

Just remember, be aware of your energy as you present. Everyone in the room can pick up on your energy, and it'll need to be invigorating to keep them interested.

Communication! Who Is It Good For?

The easy answer: communication is for *them* - your audience. It's for those who have given you their time and are waiting on your every word. If you want to become a master of public speaking, you first need to know that communication is a vital asset to have on hand. It's easy to say that it's all about body language and your tone, but this is so much more than that. Being able to have people know your name because of the presentations you give, to have a reputation as being able to communicate clearly, can make or break your career.

Communication is used to change people's minds, influence them, motivate them, and build relationships. It can easily cross language barriers and cultures. Developing your communication skills is vital to leading a fulfilled life, and should never be overlooked - even if you're honing in on it just to master public speaking. It's so much more than that! After all, so many people use communication to mend their relationships and to relay information.

You should always remember that communication is a two-way process. This is why your ability to communicate effectively is so important. I mentioned listening earlier in this chapter. Well, communication is a two-way street. You must be able to listen to your audience, even when they don't use words, and in this way, it becomes a shared experience between you and everyone in the room. When you're towards the end of your presentation, and audience feedback is part of the plan, really listening to their questions or concerns, and being able to reply properly can end the time spent together on a great note. It's an always-evolving process between you both and should be treated that way.

The Singer Who Rose Above Her Fear with A Little Help - Profile - Adele

It probably comes as a shock to learn the incredible songstress suffers from stage fright. This, of course, is the kind of woman who has sung in front of numerous audiences, including at awards shows. She's certainly one of the most popular singers in the world, so you'd think she'd be accustomed to audiences cheering her name. However, Adele has been very open about her stage fright and anxiety.

There was one incident where the singer bolted out of a fire escape rather than face a crowd. Another time she admitted to projectile puking on someone before heading out on stage. Still, despite pre-show jitters, Adele performs. But what helped her?

You'd be surprised. The singer has admitted that another singer gave her a hedge against stage fright. It was someone who she idolized before becoming famous herself. As the story goes, when Adele was about to meet Beyoncé for the first time, the shy performer almost had a panic attack. However, when Adele came face to face with Beyoncé, the mega-star gushed to Adele, "You're amazing! When I listen to you, I feel like I'm listening to God."

58

Sometimes it's the kind words of those we value that can give us the confidence to step out in front of everyone and give our best. If you're afflicted with stage fright, present to someone you trust and get a home team opinion - you might just find that a few kind words can help you when you're feeling anxious.

CHAPTER FIVE

Crafting Amazing Speeches

It doesn't matter if you're the greatest speaker in the world. If you don't have a topic that's well researched and written, your progress will have been for nothing. A mediocre speech, no matter how well recited and spoken, will not move the crowd. It won't be remembered. I'd go as far as to say it'll just leave them feeling empty.

You need to walk out onto that stage knowing that you've done everything you can to prepare yourself. You should go into it knowing that you'll keep your audience captivated - which I know you can! There are multiple techniques you can use to ensure that the people that you're speaking to will hang onto every word and start to care about what you're presenting.

Pillars of a Speech

Building a speech is a difficult process, and you want to go about it the right way. That's why I'm going to start with what you should keep in mind first. You can consider these pillars of a speech, as they deal with the public and will help you solidify what kind of speech you are wanting to create in order to get your core message across more clearly.

I know that once you begin applying either, or all, of these principles, you'll soon see a difference in the way your audience listens.

1. Persuasion

We usually think of persuasion as a bad thing. I would go so far as to say it almost sounds like a manipulative word. Persuasion has a bad rep, and shouldn't be considered as sinister as all that. When you're trying to persuade someone, after all, it is the attempt to influence someone to decide on something. You use it to change people's minds and, when it comes to speeches, it's usually backed up by facts.

You can scour the internet for one, but there are very few speeches that include even the slightest hint of persuasion. It's used more often than we think – whether it's to persuade our boss for a raise or trying to get our significant other to get along with our mother. The great thing about persuasion is that it's fluid and doesn't take just one shape. It can be molded to better your argument, whatever it might be, and it's usually not as crass as manipulation, which often uses planning and tactics to force someone to change their minds.

If you want to be persuasive, you're going to have to give everyone a reason to change their views. You can use several techniques – emotional responses, logic, or even appealing to a personal reason from your past. You want to know both sides of the argument so that you can best contrast them. This way you can present them with the argument and have them consider your stance based on the reasons you've given. It will help your cause to know both sides - that way, if anyone disagrees with you, you'll have counterpoints if you have a question segment at the end of your presentation.

2. Entertainment

I'm sure you want your speech to be entertaining no matter what, and I'm sure it will be! This is more for those speeches that are based primarily on entertainment. These are also to help you understand how to have your speech be effectively a little less boring. If you find your subject is eye-watering and tiresome, you might want to spruce it up with some entertainment.

An entertaining speech is often used to wow your audience and get their attention, while also delivering your core message. When you're focusing on entertainment, the way you speak will be different than when you're offering an informative or persuasive speech. For instance, think about the last entertaining speech you heard. Usually, we dredge up memories of toasts at weddings, or when someone is being given an award. It's not all just about the humor, either. It's about using your voice in a way that excites the audience.

Many people think that entertaining speeches can just be done on the fly. Add a little humor, maybe some funny hand gestures and stories and everyone will laugh. Well, that's not how it works. When people do this, their speeches can falter and the audience is left sitting in awkward silence. You want to put as much preparation into an entertaining speech as much as you do any other.

You want to be more open with your body language and use a lighter language. Be sure to keep things light by changing up the tone of your voice (which we get into later). You can apply small parts of entertainment in the most serious of speeches for a little liveliness, as well. You don't have to feel burdened to be entertaining—no one's expecting you to bust out a guitar and start singing Wonderwall. You just must keep in mind that entertainment can move crowds emotionally with drama, and that's something everyone loves.

3. Informing

Informative speeches are usually meant for topics that are a little more hard-hitting or for those lectures focused on specific subjects. These types of speeches are all about the facts and must convey those facts to the audience so that they're easily understood. Essentially, you're informing your audience.

There's an obvious issue with informational speeches - they're dry. It's a substantial amount of information that needs to be conveyed in a short amount of time. It really doesn't leave a lot of space for anything but the facts. It's easy to find your audience falling asleep, despite your passion for the subject. If you find it is really tedious information, you'll need to add a bit of entertainment to shock your audience away again. It's always recommended to incorporate stories, or maybe even personalize the information so that the audience can relate to the subject more easily.

The informative speech can be overwhelming, as you need to be highly organized to get all the facts crammed in. Use your citations

64

wisely and add visual aids and clues while your present. You want to get all the information into your allotted time, and visuals can be a key to cramming a lot of information into a short time without overwhelming the audience. You can always add a quick story from your own life in there, and you should be well within your time, so long as you organize everything and practice beforehand.

It's always important to keep even dull subject matter interesting. What you have to say matters! So, for the best informative speeches, always mix in a little of either entertainment or persuasion. This is one of the speech pillars that need help from the others because, although important, it can grow dull quickly.

4. Well-Defined Message

Your speech is your message - so make sure it's well defined. The way you craft your speech is integral to the way it's taken by the audience and considered important to them. Consider yourself as the initiator of a conversation, and you want them to get in on it. You make it easy enough for them to understand, while also being able to connect with it, and you'll not only hold their attention, but you'll have them intrigued.

So, how do you define a message? It depends entirely on what you're trying to convey, but it's an overarching theme that can be used for any kind of public speaking engagement you may have. There are a few questions you can use to help you define your message.

- Who is your audience?

- What do you want them to learn?

- How can you make what you're saying integral to them, while also staying true to the keynotes?

- How many people will be there?

- What is the time limit?

Consider all these things while determining your message. You need to make your message as clear as possible, and these questions will help you figure out your key points. You want all your points to be subsets of your defining message - which is why it's so important to develop one in the first place.

You can choose to open your presentation with your message, or you can choose to deliver it after a number of points, making it clear to the crowd just what they're in for. Now, knowing which to choose will be based on what your message is, of course. You also want to be comfortable with the placement. Definitely don't choose something that will make you unsure! If you choose to open with your message too quickly and get lost along the way, you might lose your audience - so keep it straightforward and be smart about the placement.

The Ultimate Beginning

The first few moments are the most important! Studies have found that a first impression lasts only seven seconds - so the time you spend in the beginning is crucial to winning your audience. There are multiple ways you can begin a presentation or a speech - whichever you choose should, as mentioned before, be one you're comfortable with. It should be known that each one will have a different effect on your audience and knowing this effect will leave a lasting impression for the rest of your presentation.

Storytelling

Public speaking is an art form, and using your words to create or refer to a personal story can be a great way to connect with the crowd. There is a rule to this, though - don't, and I repeat, don't interrupt your speech or presentation with your story. Don't start your presentation and then stop just to tell the story. You want it to be streamlined into it so that it weaves seamlessly, as this way it won't distract everyone from your main message. The story option is an effective opener. Since infanthood, it has thrilled us when we hear the beginnings of a story - so make sure it's an entertaining one!

Example: "I was like you once, just a teenager. I spent my days skipping school and hanging out with bad people. Drugs were rampant with this group, and it led me to do some awful things."

Ask Away

First, if you open with a question, you want to give a statement or a what-if scenario. Not only will this get the crowd thinking, but it'll get their attention. This is a strong opener because it gets everyone involved from the moment you start.

Example: "It's said that only ten percent of the people in our world find the key to happiness. It takes a lot of key steps to finding your own happiness. Are you willing to put in the work so that you, too, can achieve a level of bliss that spills into every facet of your life?"

Make A Statement

Nothing gets a person's attention like a statement that pertains to them. If you're looking to get people hooked on every word, you can choose to make a statement that relates to each person in the room. The statement doesn't need to be negative - but it should pertain to your core message and fit in with the research you've made. Be sure to mention whichever source you've chosen, if there is research involved. You don't want everyone in the room thinking that you're making things up.

Example: "Global warming is not slowing. In fact, it affects all of us. It's been discovered that we've had our 16th warmest year in NASA's 134-year temperature study."

Be Thankful

This is a great way to start, as you're showing humility and gratitude. If you're speaking to a venue, you must thank those who've organized it for you, as well as thanking the audience for attending. You actually end up making everyone in the room feel important and excited for the presentation to come.

Example: "To start, I'd like to thank everyone for coming today. It's important to me that you've all arrived and thank you to the coordinators for making this happen. Can we get a round of applause for everyone who helped put this together today?"

Be Complementary

It might come across as sucking up, but it helps everyone see you as someone willing to listen and observe everyone in the room. By complimenting them, you're making your message more about them than yourself - and it makes a fantastic first impression.

Example: "So, to start, I'd like to say that it's been a pleasure working with you throughout the years. I know that this presentation applies to all of us, especially since I've been able to get to know all of you well during our work hours."

Using Imagination

Imagination is endless - use it to your advantage! This brings everyone into a cohesive feeling where they can visualize a situation together. Not only will it give you some respite before jumping into your presentation, but it'll help you connect with everyone in the room.

Example: "Imagine you're standing in front of your boss, and you've just been told you've had a raise. Feel that feeling, and now open your eyes. Success is what we make it."

Your Speech Outline

This part will be intensive, but I know you can handle it! Once you've mastered your body language and tone your words are your next vital key to delivering a perfect presentation. Your speech outline will make it so you're organized and understand your key points. This will be what you must memorize to the best of your abilities before you go up in front of the crowd. I know from personal experience that having an unorganized outline can lead to an increasingly difficult presentation.

There are multiple parts to an outline, and each should be dependent on the other. You want to transition them properly so that you're not repeating information. Each key point serves its own purpose and has its place. Listed below are some guidelines to follow so that you can ensure that your outline is perfect for your public speaking event.

Part One - Introduce Yourself

You need to start with a bang - so be sure to use at least one of the concepts listed in this chapter. I want your audience to be wowed the moment you step out onto that stage or into that boardroom. No matter where you are, you should start with a strong intro so that everyone is automatically listening. Feel free to use some of the introductions offered in this chapter and adapt them to your own presentation.

The introduction has a number of key parts that you want to follow. These are listed in order as they are the first parts. Some are optional, but others are key to beginning your speech. Each one that's considered optional will be stated. Follow them in order and you're sure to come up with a perfect introduction.

Grab Their Attention

The first sentence you utter sets the tone for the rest of the presentation. It's vital to how the rest of it will unfold, so be sure that the first thing you say will impact your audience. It's been proven that you have less than twenty seconds to make a first impression. It can't be changed after that, so be sure to use an opening sentence that reflects your core message, but also grabs their attention.

Establish Credibility

If you're speaking to an unfamiliar crowd, give them a reason to listen to you. Tell them why you're the person to speak to them on the subject. Giving them some background, either about your knowledge on the subject or through a story of your personal life, you can have them believe the words you're saying.

Core Message

This is where you introduce the message of your entire speech. You want to let them know why they're there. This is great if you're speaking publicly about a specific topic, especially an opinion. If you're giving a presentation to your work colleagues, this is where you'd tell them the main focus of your research, whether it's the new product or changing a policy in the departments. You want to have a core message and a good introduction to it. This will be what you build your key points on.

Preview of Presentation

This step is optional and can help you if you have a longer presentation. It can also set the stage so that everyone knows what they can expect from you throughout the time allotted. Here you would place a short slide or offer a quick overview of what they can expect. This is especially useful if you have a longer presentation on an intensive subject that has a variable of points.

Part Two - Key Points and Subpoints

Your part two comes directly after your introduction, so make sure you transition smoothly between your beginning into your key points. After you've given your central idea and message, you can then get to the key points or the reasons as to why your core message is what it is. You want to have primarily one point per slide and then subpoints that help you prove them. These will lend credibility to your message, so be sure the main portion of part two should be your subpoints. These will help you to maintain a focus on your message.

Now, you can use as many key points as you need - just be sure to back up your information with proper research and citations! If you're applying any statistics or information from a survey, be sure to mention where you got it from. You don't have to put this information in the slideshow or presentation itself, you just need to say it.

Part Three - Argue for Your Message

It's all about the contrast! If you're trying to convince the crowd of your point, be sure to use contrasting arguments and refuting them. You want to do this before the last part of your presentation so that they leave on the note that your core message is correct. Applying these too early in the presentation might cause the audience to forget, especially if you have a lot of information that you need to relay to the crowd.

When you use contrasting points in your presentation, you'll find that it captures the attention of your audience. It surprises them and makes them consider the subject matter – particularly because when you're contrasting something, it adds a sense of drama. The more you sustain their attention, the more they'll remember your core message. Using contrasting points also adds facts to your words by placing them next to differing ideas. It helps everyone in the crowd understand your point of view a little more if you can offer examples.

There are three parts to a contrasting argument – first is your core message, which should be the first thing you discuss. You want to talk about all the implications of why they need to take your message into account. The second part is analyzing the outcome, and why the current method doesn't work. You then finish with the positives about your message and how it can change things.

Example:

Step 1 - *Taxes need to be raised on the rich. It will help us develop better communities and bring about better housing and necessities for our areas.*

Step 2 - *Without taxing the rich, they'll only get what? Richer. This is how things are now – they have a number of assets that they don't need.*

Step 3 - *So, when we look at taxing the rich, you'll see that we can put that money into different areas, such as schools and transportation. If we do this sooner, we can see changes made quicker.*

I want it to be known that that's just an example. I'm contrasting two points, while also making you consider my message. I give you reasons and then elaborate on them. Of course, your presentation won't be so minimal, but you get the idea. It makes you wonder what more could be said, and if it's a possibility. That's the beauty of contrasting ideas.

Part Four - Say It Again for the People in the Back

Part four is directly before your conclusion, which should be a separate part altogether. You can use this part to summarize your key points and core message. This is a basic formula for a speech or presentation but is always effective. You can always choose to change things slightly, especially if you're looking to create a unique presentation.

In this last part, be sure to capture the attention of the audience. This is towards the conclusion, and you want them to leave your presentation understanding everything they've just heard. So, if you are summarizing a heavy amount of information, try to really narrow it down to the most important points and keep it minimal so that it's easier to understand. You should consider your summary more like an explanation.

Conclusion - Say Your Last Words

I want you to think about some of your favorite movies. What was it about them that really grabbed your attention? Why do you love them? For some people, it's the way the movie ends. When a truly great movie reaches its climax, everyone in the audience is moved to silence. I want you to be able to finish your presentations and speeches with such a feeling. There are ways to have your last words to be just as memorable as the first.

Besides, there might be times when your message gets lost in the ruckus in the middle of the speech. Maybe you accidentally lost your way? No need to worry. You can end it on the right note and have your core message be the last thing people leave the room with.

Challenge Them

Were you looking to stir action into the crowd? If you were, we all know that there's nothing like a challenge to get them to feel that they, too, need to act. It's a sort of call to action. If you start your conclusion with your main message and then tell them what they can do to change the outcome or even their own lives.

Compare

If you're given a speech about something that needs to be changed, then a great way to end it is to compare the thing you're against. You'll possibly have already done this in part three. However, if you're looking to convince them to change their minds, it's a great way to remind them. This will have the audience question the validity of the opposition. For example, you can say, "we either destroy the Earth with global warming, or we build a future for our children." Not only are you reinforcing your message, but you're leaving the audience on a note of the change.

Storytime

Do you want to have them speak about your presentation as they leave? End it with humor. Nothing sets up a crowd to leave with smiles on their faces like ending with a joke. You can always choose a joke that has aspects of your core message embedded into it, or one that repeats a key point that you'll have made earlier. If you do choose this conclusion, be sure to use the joke on a friend or two to determine whether it's actually funny. The last thing you want to do is end with silence and crickets in the room.

Thank you, Thank you

I'm sure you already know where I'm going with this! You want to make it clear to everyone in the room that you've finished. This is a casual, but humble way to end your presentation. You simply thank the audience for listening and attending - this is a simple but effective way to finish. It's been done many times but it never really gets old because people always feel appreciative of someone recognizing their time spent to hear your message.

Visual Stimuli

Have you given your closing statement? Well, this would be a great time to impact the audience. To do this, you can always use an image that makes the crowd think. So, choose an image that refers to your message, and that makes your crowd sit for a minute or two before leaving and gives them think.

The Business Mogul Who Overcame His Fear - Profile - Warren Buffett

There's a good chance you've heard the man's name. After all, he's one of the richest men in the world. He's likely attended more meetings and presentations than we will in our entire lives, seeing as he's the CEO of Berkshire Hathaway and an investor. There's no doubt people pitch

76

to him every day. As a businessman, though, he's had to pitch or present to others. Unfortunately, in his early career, Warren Buffet was terrified of public speaking.

The business mogul is open about his early stage fright, and how it impacted his career. It could be said that if he didn't overcome his fears, he may not have become the man we've all heard of today. So, how did he do it?

You may be surprised he followed steps similar to what I've laid out in this book you're reading now. He's even admitted to taking a public speaking course, only to drop out because he was too nervous! There's no doubt he had many obstacles to overcome, and he did it one step at a time.

The billionaire signed up for a public speaking course and, after graduating, began to speak as a lecturer at a local college. He started by exposing himself to possibilities where he'd need to rely on his public speaking. He also began to practice alone, trying to get into the mindset that he could stand in front of that crowd without ruining his lecture.

Although he didn't realize it, Warren Buffett faced his fears and did it anyway. It's likely because of this that he's become the fearless business magnate he is today. There's no way to tell, of course, but he's certainly come a long way since being that young man who was too terrified to even stand before a crowd.

CHAPTER SIX

Designing a Stellar Presentation

You should use the outline from the previous chapter to focus on the first part of your presentation. This part, however, is going to be all about how to make a presentation. This includes what tools you can use, data visualizations, and finding the words to emphasize your message to the audience. I have no doubt that your presentation, after using some of the options in this chapter, will wow the people in the room.

Tools to Use

Having the right presentation starts with having the right program to create your slideshow. There's one popular presentation creator that most companies use - Microsoft PowerPoint. It's synonymous with presentations but it's not your only option. I've listed below several different slide presentation programs that might just suit what you need! Beyond that, I've included only programs that can be downloaded for free.

Google Slides

Using this online option is effective when you need to work on your presentation from anywhere. You won't need a USB or a particular computer, either. You can work on it on any device because your file will be kept on your Google account. This option is also great when you're working with a group, as anyone in the group will be able to adjust your presentation as you go along. You can allow access to the document to certain people.

Keynote

Are you an Apple fan? If you are, then Keynote should become your preferred program. This is because this program is best used with iCloud, iOS, and Mac devices. Like many of the ones listed here, this is an easy program to adapt to. It comes with a variety of different options, such as using it on multiple devices, special effects for your presentation, and unique themes that you can customize. One of the downsides is that this program is only available on Apple devices.

Photostage Slideshow Software

You'll find this program to be one of the easiest to use. It allows for the seamless creation of professional slideshows and also has a variety of editing options. Like most slideshow applications, you can include pictures, transitions, and music. You can also turn the slideshow into a DVD, if necessary, or upload it to YouTube for easy streaming from anywhere.

Movavi Slideshow Maker

This is an easy program, and it allows you to create personalized slideshows with a variety of different options. The real winning point to this program is the premade slideshow templates and library of free background music, filters, and special effects. This is the program you'd want to use if you're looking to create a presentation that has more customization options. It's the best program for a more unique slideshow.

Building Your Slideshow

What makes a good slideshow into an outstanding slideshow? I want you to think of a few things you notice immediately when you're looking at a presentation. Is it its appeal visually? Is it the words that are chosen? Maybe how the information is displayed? Let me tell you one thing - it's everything combined. To create a slideshow that not only shows your information correctly but also is aesthetically pleasing isn't as easy as it may sound. You don't just click a few buttons on the screen and suddenly have it all figured out.

There are certain steps you can take to create a slideshow worthy of your subject, while also being aesthetic. You can avoid the kind of presentation that people tend to look away from by using these steps, which gives you a guideline to go by. Feel free to adapt it - just know that you should keep each step and not throw any that aren't optional away.

Outline

It goes without saying, but you should always outline your presentation before you start creating it in the program. After all, you need to know what you're going to say. No matter how much information you put into each slide, if you're just winging it, chances are it'll come out as messy and unprofessional. To do an outline, just write down the information you want to appear on each slide and divide it up between the subject matter. You'll have already created an outline for the entirety of your presentation, so you can use that as a basis and then place the information in order into the slideshow.

Here is just one example of an outline for a slideshow presentation:

1. Introduction

2. Core Message

3. Proposition (or Summary)

4. Why They Should Consider the Proposition (Key Points)

5. More Reasons to Consider (Examples of Key Points)

6. Conclusion

7. Thanks/Questions

This is just a basic presentation. Each one doesn't include just one slide, as there might be multiple key points or reasons to consider with your topic, especially if it's a comparison statement. It doesn't matter how many you need to use - just make sure the information is clear and concise on each slide.

Tone

You'll need to set the tone depending on what type of presentation you're doing. Now, if you're going for a professional tone, for example, you won't want to go with a snowman theme (obviously). You'll also want to use jargon related to your field of work, whatever it might be. If your presentation is humorous, you'll want to set your slideshow up so that it has lighter colors so that everyone knows what to expect right away. You shouldn't be too wary of not using a specific tone that's a variation of what you typically see. This is your slideshow, so feel free to make it unique, while also staying in the realm of what tone you're setting. Professional meetings can be informal, so don't worry and make the experience enjoyable for everyone - even if the information might be a little dry.

Utilize Your Key Points

Your main points should be the focus of your talk. Not only will they help you remember specific aspects of your subject, but they'll help you with timing your information properly so that you don't veer off. You should always make a list of your key points that revolve around your core message. You should have cues embedded in your presentation so that you can jog your memory in case you lose your way or forget a specific thing. When considering your main points, you should classify them properly – whether you're doing a professional presentation or a speaking engagement. Titling them is important, as you can make them serious or humorous.

Don't forget to back them up with sub-points. We'll get into that later, but you want each point to be clarified with proper information. You can then use this data to substantiate your core message and prove your point, no matter what it is.

Your Visuals Speak for You

There are certain colors that the eyes naturally gravitate to, but it's not just about placing these colors wherever. When you're building a slideshow for your presentation, you always want to follow simple rules to have it capture everyone's attention. After all, we may not always judge a book by a cover, but that's only for books. The way your presentation appears will have your audience's eyes, so make sure they have something nice to look at.

Visual Style

You can always use a template, but that looks kind of lazy - especially if someone recognizes it! God forbid that happen. So, instead, you should build your own theme so that you can choose your own style and colors. One thing you don't want to do is have many different styles throughout your presentation. This is likely to get everyone's attention, and not for good reasons. It'll be a distraction if anything else. You want your slides to be streamlined and to follow a certain style that you've chosen. So, keep it consistent throughout the whole slideshow. This includes any text boxes or charts you might use - keep the color scheme the same throughout.

Leave Some Space

No one likes clutter. Whether it's on your desk or in your home, it's a jumbled mess that doesn't appeal to the eye. Make sure you keep your slides clutter-free! Less is always more when it comes to your presentation. You should use your words, rather than adding all the words you're going to say to your slides. You want the others in the room to be listening rather than reading the entire time, otherwise, you could have just emailed it to them.

Colors Are A Crowds' Best Friend

Say hello to one of the main setups for your slideshow. If you use colors properly, you'll discover that the style will truly come together. If you work for a company, there may be specific colors you can use - so use them wisely! If you're just looking to present an original idea, be sure to choose colors that go together well and contrast the other. Try to avoid colors that look too similar to each other, like indigo and navy. You want there to be a flow to your slideshow. For example, blue and white and contrasting colors that feed off each other well and still appeal to the eye.

When choosing your font color, you want to stick to something dark that will make it so that everyone can read them. Don't use bright colors! If you use a light color on a dark background, such as yellow on black, it might look unprofessional. If you are dead-set on using a light color on a dark background, only make your font white. If the font is narrow stroked, make the face bold so the image is clearly legible. Also, avoid using too many words on a single slide, the audience can't read that fast and listen and watch you. Stay away from the red font, as it will appear as though everything is written wrong. Red is the typical color for marking mistakes, so everyone will subconsciously apply it to your presentation.

If you're unsure of how many colors you should use, it's always best to stick to a smaller amount. So, try to only have about two or three to start - you can always change it if you feel like it looks a little bland.

Choose two opposing colors, such as white and black, and then a secondary color to add some definition.

Charts and Diagrams

Charts are an easy way to get information across without having to say out the numbers or list them, which can be an eyesore. Be mindful of how you use color, and make the information in the charts clear enough so everyone can understand it just from seeing it. Only add charts that are important to the subject at hand - you don't want to overwhelm them with data. It's also best if you don't add too many numbers or text alongside your chart, as it can be cluttered. You can always say the details of the chart, too, instead of adding an abundant amount of numbers in the slide.

Charts to consider and they're best uses:

- Column chart - this chart is best used when you're comparing multiple subjects. You might choose to add in a few different dates, products, or options for your work. The information you add in is up to you, but using this chart will help you easily relay the information so that everyone can see the differences.

- Scatter chart - use this one if you're comparing numbers, usually meant for sales or consensus. If you have innumerable subjects, this one's your best bet. It's usually used for comparing locations, or dates and for the many different subjects you may have.

- Stacked column charts - this one's best for composition. Use a maximum of four composition items so that the chart doesn't appear too big in the slideshow.

Animation and Transitions

Be careful when using animations and transitions! You don't want your slideshow to look unprofessional which can happen - especially if you're adding a ridiculous amount of animation in each slide. You want to use animations to add style to your slideshow and add to the content involved. Make sure that it's not distracting, but rather appeals to the eye and blends into the slideshow effortlessly. If you're doing a company presentation, take it easy and make the transitions slow. One of the best ways to incorporate animation is to reveal your sub-points that relate to your key points or to go from one subject to another while transitioning slides.

Finding the Words

We've all had to sit through a bad presentation. Let me ask you this: what do you think constitutes a bad presentation? It's often all in the words we use. This doesn't include just when we're speaking, but it's also based on what we're looking at. Usually, these are also presentations that are longer than they need to be and aren't visually stimulating.

Your audience, whether they know it or not, are picky about the text that appears in your slideshow. Typically, they'll respond best to presentations that offer visuals and minimal text. They tend to be more engaged with these types of slideshow presentations. Not only do you not bombard them with a ridiculous amount of information, but you also leave some out, which is great for getting them to ask questions.

You wouldn't want your audience reading a book, so know that it can be overwhelming to them when they're confronted with a wall of text. It's like trying to read a thesis – no one wants to do that. It will often confuse everyone because they expect to *hear* the information rather than read it. Therefore, you should only include the necessary information. Leave yourself space to explain each part of your key points.

This is why you'll want to focus on your core message. Make sure that each slide communicates your message by adding information to its key points (this is also why outlining your slideshow is vital to the success of your presentation). Once you focus on your message, it'll be easier to get across with fewer words.

So, bring on the edits! You'll want to get rid of any excess information. Finish your slides and then, with a stern eye, edit the crap out of them. If there's information in there that doesn't need to be seen, just delete it. You can always say the information rather than having it on the slide. You want to go for a minimalistic look – think in bullet points, then elaborate yourself and add informational graphs so that they can understand if there are numbers involved.

I know how difficult it can be to cut the information down, especially when you're passionate about the subject, but you shouldn't keep any extra wording that doesn't add to your presentation. Let your passion show with what you say, rather than what you show on the screen. This also keeps you from repeating anything, as you'll have the points to keep you in check. When you go overboard with the wording in your presentation, you may unknowingly repeat yourself a few times, which will only make it seem as though you didn't spend enough time on it.

Wrapping It Up

First off, you want to put it all together far before the date when you'll present. This will help you be better prepared and give you enough time to practice. The better rehearsed you are, the more natural the presentation will be.

You want your core message to be important to you and you want to find reasons to be passionate about it. You can always feign interest, but you'll lose your audiences that way. They'll pick up that you're not that interested regardless of how enthusiastic you might pretend to be. So, make sure that you've chosen things that you enjoy and then everyone that you're presenting to will enjoy it as well. This goes for your titles, your slides, and your visuals. If everything comes together so that you're pleased, that'll reflect onto the audience.

Build on your central theme and make sure your presentation encompasses that. I'm sure there'll be nerves beforehand—it happens to even the best of us. But if your presentation is ready, all the information is put together properly, and you've given yourself time to rehearse, there's a good chance you'll soar.

How A Golf Great Overcame His Stutter - Profile - Tiger Woods

Tiger Woods is a household name, and he's a living golf legend. He also had a stutter he had to get through to become the person he is today. He credits his competitiveness in every aspect of his life as something that has helped him overcome his difficulty in forming words. There have been interviews where his stutter returns.

But how did he do it? The answer will probably surprise you. Not only was it his enduring ability to work through it, but it was also being able to speak to his dog. He would practice speaking to his dog until the good boy would fall asleep.

"I finally learned how to do that, without stuttering all over myself," he said, without so much as a pause.

Stuttering stems from childhood and can be difficult to overcome. There are speech therapies and schools that help students defeat their way of talking. Sometimes, though, it takes a little practice and a best friend to help you deal with your fear of speaking in front of others - no matter what the reason.

CHAPTER SEVEN

Successfully Attract Your Audience

There's something different about public speakers. Somehow, they're able to stand in front of a crowd, speak to them, and move them to action. If you want to master public speaking, there's more to it than just being able to entertain. You have to be able to motivate them too and have them *really* listen to you. Your audience will appreciate you for it and being able to do so will allow you to create a network of people that can help you build a strong career later down the line. By speaking with that magnetism that brings people in, you'll likely end up booking extra speaking engagements through word of mouth.

This is all about being a magnet and drawing people into what you're saying with your voice, your words, and your body language. It's a trifecta that, when brought together, can change the way you hold yourself on stage. It also changes the way people react to you, no matter what subject you're speaking on. Once you understand that each gesture and each word will have a different effect, you can then work on your presence. This is where you do the work on the inside so that it can radiate from you - which I know it can!

Lead the Way

I want you to think of someone you know that has a commanding presence. Now, this can be a celebrity or someone you know - it doesn't matter. Try to think of what it is that brings you in when they speak or when they enter a room. Do your eyes follow them? Do you hang onto every word they say? This can be considered the *je ne sais quoi* factor. You'd think that they were born with it, but it's often something that's built through life experiences and natural leadership skills. Want to know the best part? You can learn how to harness this so that you can develop your own *je ne sais quoi* factor every time you enter a room and present.

All About Interest

Sure, you can learn to speak and woo a crowd. That's fine. Do you know what isn't? Not listening to feedback when someone else is speaking. The best way to gain other people's respect is to not only be interesting but to also be interested in what they say.

I used to have a bad habit of scanning the room out of nervousness when someone was speaking to me. My eyes would jump from person to person, as though I was waiting for a new opportunity for a new conversation, even if that wasn't the case. How do you think that made the person speaking feel? I can only imagine they felt pretty awful and wanted to finish that conversation as quickly as possible.

I've since learned to make eye contact and *really* listen to what people have to say. This includes when you're the center of attention and onstage. If someone has a question or wants to give some feedback, take a moment to let them speak and finish their sentences. Don't interrupt them - just listen. If you show that you're interested, they'll be interested too.

Strength - Not the Muscle Kind

Do you know your strengths? If you don't, you definitely should! After all, each public speaker is distinct and will have a flare in varying ways. I want you to figure out what your strengths are so you can play to them and enhance your public speaking abilities. It's not always about how you can just talk to a crowd - it can be so many other things! Do people think you're funny? Are you great at telling stories? Do you have a calming presence with new people? These are just some of the things you can consider before you write down your strengths. Look over them and think of ways you can apply these strengths and enhance your presentation.

Use Your Experiences

Instead of using sentences like, "you might understand", or "if this happened to you once". That won't get your audience fully involved with your presentation. Instead, use the experiences you've had in your own life as examples. Sure, this can be a little intimidating. I have no doubt that you'll feel naked at first, and that's okay. But here's a fun fact - everyone will relate to you. Want to know why? We're all human. We may not have the exact same life experiences, but most of us have shared emotions relating to your own life stories. There's a part of us in each of them and, in that way, we're all similar. So, use your stories, and you'll see that a spark will show up within the crowd as they start to see themselves while you speak your truth.

Don't Fear Silence

Whenever we watch a movie, you'll notice that the entire audience is silent. We get frustrated if someone starts talking in the middle of an important scene. If your speaking and the crowd remains silent, don't get overexcited or nervous. This is often a good sign.

As a speaker, you'll run into these situations often. The room might be so quiet that you can hear a pencil drop or someone coughs in the back. I want you to embrace the silence. You might even want to pause and let the silence seep into the room, creating a type of surmounting tension before you begin speaking again. If you show that you have a grasp of the silence, you'll find that you come across as more confident. Normally nervous speakers try to laugh their way out of the stillness of a crowd or try to fill it with their voice. Do the opposite and you'll gain the respect of the people in the room without them even knowing.

Be Authentic

One thing you might notice about the many ways to emphasize leadership skills while presenting is all about listening, donning your strengths like armor, and speaking from experience. What's the one thing they all have in common? Authenticity. Let that sink in. *You* are worthy of being authentic in front of a crowd. You are enough and I know that people will want to hear what you have to say. Sometimes, though, it's all about the way we say it. This is why I know the concepts in this book will help you reveal your true self and make you feel at ease while public speaking. Often, it's all about being truthful to who we are. Maybe it's why we fear being in front of a crowd - we're essentially alone. Let me tell you this: it's not always a bad thing.

When you think of the famous speeches ever written, it wasn't always about the words, as moving as they may be. What we remember is usually how it was said. It was the way Martin Luther King, Jr. said, "I have a dream," that brought people to bring their hands together and clap. The way he spoke was true to his authentic self. When we see something that bores us, it's not always because the person speaking is nervous – sometimes it's because they hate what they're doing. They're just going with the motions. They don't want to be there, so you don't want to be there. If you find yourself being one of those people, try to find something about the subject matter you're covering (especially if it's for a job) and get passionate about it. When you're authentic about your excitement, other people will sense that off you and start to feel it, too.

This is an important leadership quality because authenticity makes people want to be around you. When you start to be authentic and speak your mind in a way that really tries to come from a place of understanding, it's hard to question what you've said. I've been in the industry for over a decade – this is one of those attributes that lie at the core of most public speakers whose names you can list off the top of your head. I know how difficult it is to get to that place, though.

Sometimes, in fact, it can feel impossible. I'm going to tell you why it isn't, and why your authentic self matters!

Finding Your Authentic Voice

I know there's the fear of seeming as though you're just speaking from a sheet. We've all seen those presentations with cue cards, where the presenter shuffles it around in their hands, searching for the next thing to say. These don't communicate to your audience that you're there to wow them – this is why authenticity is such an asset. You certainly don't want to lose your credibility in the eyes of those who've come to see you present.

Why do you connect to your core message? Really consider it. Why is it important to you? You might just be presenting a product to a client, or doing a wedding toast, but it doesn't matter. You've been given the task to speak to a crowd. You need to make a connection to the statement you're trying to make and apply it yourself. In essence, it's not always about what you're speaking publicly about. It's how it relates to you. After all, if you relate it to yourself, you can also relate it to the audience. When you consider it this way your words then become your truth.

But how do you determine this? You must know who you are. This doesn't just mean your life story - it's deeper than that. Where do you see yourself in the world? When you can start answering this kind of question, you can find your identity. You can then connect unique things to your passions, what you don't like, or even how it pertains to your everyday routine.

You don't want to lie or be inconsistent. People can tell when you're lying. It's like when you walk out of a change room, look to the salesperson, and ask them if it looks good. When they reply with a lie, you can tell - you don't end up buying the product. It's the exact same concept as standing in front of a crowd and being inauthentic. They can tell. So, incorporate yourself into the presentation. You'll be surprised by the reaction you get.

Practicing Authenticity

There's no doubt that practicing before a speaking engagement is crucial to being able to deliver a good speech. However, you don't want to sound overly rehearsed. One of the ways you can avoid this is by forcing yourself to do gestures that you're uncomfortable with. You do want to maintain eye contact with your audience – but *don't* creep them out! You don't want to have a staring contest with the person in the front row all because you're trying to watch your body language. *Do* be aware of what your body is doing, but don't be too forceful – everyone in the room will be able to tell if you are.

You're probably wondering, *how do I become authentic, then*? Sure, body language was already mentioned in this book. It's a subtle way of communicating with your audience, and its importance to your presentation can't be overstated. If you want to create an authentic feel to your presentation or your speech, you'll want to practice while considering the audience. If you practice your gestures too much, they might come off as robotic.

There are some rules you can use to help you rehearse to perfection, while also maintaining your authenticity. You want to listen, be excited about what you're talking about, and always be facing the audience with an open stance. If you can do these, there's a better chance of you succeeding. You can use these three rules to rehearse and practice gestures. Feel free to use a mirror if you're unsure.

Variety Show

Okay, so you have a boring topic. You've read the book up until this point and you're staring at the pages, thinking, "what if I need to sell a vacuum cleaner to a multimillionaire?" Well, that doesn't sound very fun - especially if it's not your vacuum cleaner. I'm sure doing a presentation on suction isn't the greatest way to go about your day, but you need to get it done. And I know you can do it! This is where you bring in variety, and spice up your presentation so that both you and everyone in the room don't fall asleep.

Add Some Sparks

You have a boring topic - it doesn't mean it gives you a pass at being a boring speaker! You might be nearly crying from a breakdown because you hate what you have to present, but it's all about using a different angle to make it more entertaining. So, stop staring at a blank screen and boring presentation. We're about to fix it.

You can think of it from a strategic point of view - what angle do I take to make this interesting? Many people approach topics that aren't that interesting from different angles, to find one that suits their needs in an entertaining way.

Disrupt It

I'm definitely not talking about jumping up and down while suddenly juggling. Obviously. We usually think of disruptions as bad things, but it can actually draw attention back if the crowd has begun to lose interest. It's essentially about surprising everyone in the room. This will not only have their eyes on you but they'll keep them there.

This works best if you have a boring and flat presentation, as disrupting it will regain the crowd's attention. It's all about breaking up the flow of your words with entertainment. At one point in the presentation, you can stop and surprise the audience with something new – whether it's a survey, a graphic, a quote, or even a video.

You want to make sure it's relevant to the topic. Once you see that the material, which might be dry, has taken its course, you can do an impromptu questionnaire. This will bring them back to your presentation and get them involved. Remember, you want it to flow. Make your disruption necessary to continue with your topic.

Relatability

A great way to get your audience involved is to check social media trends. You can give your subject relevance by relating it to something happening in the world at that very moment. Check out popular trends happening in the world and adapt a part of your presentation to it. You can even allow a debate to get started where you compare your subject to something relevant happening right now. Not only will this get people's attention, but it'll get them riled up, too. Just be sure to use something that relates to the content in some way. I also recommend being careful of what you choose, as you don't want to get the crowd riled up because you've done something offensive.

Metaphorically Speaking

If you have a dry subject that might be hard to understand, you can always use metaphors during your presentation to make it more interesting and to get everyone thinking. When you use a metaphor, you're asking a rhetorical question that the audience can answer in their heads. The idea isn't to give them the answer - have them do that for themselves. So, you can ask them, what is it like? Or, if you were to compare it to these things, which would it be, to you? You allow them to elaborate on the subject on their own, which gives them the independence they need to figure out your subject for themselves, rather than being forced to know it offhand.

Have the Answers

One thing you'll notice about people that naturally attract people to them is that they're never afraid to say what's on their minds. When you're standing on stage, this might be a difficult thing to do, as you've rehearsed for hours, if not days.

If you've chosen to end your speech or presentation with a Q and A, you might find that you'll hit a snag in the road when people start coming up with questions you weren't prepared for. I'm sure you've come across someone who comes up with a one-worded answer whenever you speak to them. Whenever this happens, you can't help but think to yourself that there's not much substance there. So, when you've decided to end with questions, make a list of answers that you can use.

When you choose your answers, make sure they have depth and personality. Research until you can't research anymore, or add some anecdotes from your own life if you're unsure. Offering a true and authentic response will help others see you as more personally available to them. It's an amazing tool to utilize, as it's highly overlooked. Most people don't expect such thoughtful answers. You can not only leave on a good note, but you'll make an impression on them right before they leave the venue or board room.

Magnetism Comes from Within

I can only imagine that you'll feel like a fraud at first, as though you're faking your way through becoming a more magnetic person, as though you're trying to manipulate your way into getting people to like you. This is how it starts but soon you'll notice shifts in your own attitude and personality.

Your magnetism comes from within. This is the *je ne sais quoi* factor. It's not about what's on the outside because, as attractive as you might be, you need to work on the inside. If you're the most attractive person in the world but you don't have amiable qualities on the inside, you'll find that people will walk away just as quickly as they walked in. Magnetism is being your authentic self, being considerate for others, choosing your words, and possessing self-control. These are not only incredible leadership qualities but they're qualities the world needs more of.

It'll lead you to the right kind of magnetism that'll outside even the worst of presentations. This isn't to say that you can just wing it on stage, but your ability to connect to a crowd will be amplified. I know that it'll take some practice, but I have no doubt that you'll be able to be your true self and allow others to see the wonderful aspects that make you who you are.

The Actor Who Stepped Up Despite His Fears - Profile - Harrison Ford

You know him as Han Solo and Indiana Jones. This incredible actor has been famous for over 30 years so you'd think he'd get used to speaking in front of strangers. His job is to literally perform in front of dozens of people - action scenes included. So how does someone like him suffer from a fear of public speaking?

Despite his incredible career on screen, Harrison Ford has admitted that public speaking fills him with "terror and anxiety". It was when he went to receive the Life Achievement Award of the American Film Institute, Harrison admitted having issues giving his speech.

He spoke to journalists saying that, "the greatest fear in my life is public speaking." What did he do then? He still went up. Despite his fears, Harrison walked up onto that stage, gave a speech, and accepted his award. The only thing you can do is just go up there and do it, despite the nerves and anxiety.

It also doesn't help if you're accepting an award – that makes it a little bit nicer afterward.

CHAPTER EIGHT

Avoiding Self-Sabotages

There's one great thing about mistakes - you learn from them! But what if you already knew what mistakes you shouldn't make? Then you can avoid them. This isn't like avoiding fear - this is about being prepared. To be prepared, you need to know what not to do and what not to include in your presentations. I want you to succeed with each public speaking engagement you have, especially by avoiding the mistakes I, and many others, have made before.

About the Audience

If you're not talking to an audience, you're talking to an empty room. Keep this in mind when you're presenting. Your audience makes you a public speaker. Without them, you won't have anyone to relay your information to. The following mistakes will make you upset or lose your audience - be sure to keep them out of your presentation. I want you to gain an audience as you go, so avoid the mistakes that can cause angst while you're public speaking.

Information Overload

I can remember when I first started public speaking. I wanted the crowd to know just how much I knew about gaining confidence. I was standing there with the glare of the lights in my face and the silence of the crowd in front of me and I went ten minutes over the time when I was supposed to finish. I had seven key points broken down into three subsections each. I told them about body language and voice and cited all the studies - there were lots of charts involved. Can you guess what happened? Some of them left, and I even saw two of them falling asleep. I learned from that moment that, although I was prepared, I had let my core message down.

When you spend too much time on the information and not enough on the message, you end up losing your audience. You want to say everything concisely - keep it simple. You'll always hold their attention if you make your points and move on. I can think of a few teachers who went on and on about certain subjects and eventually we'd all start passing notes to each other because we weren't paying attention. This is the kind of thing that happens when you're droning on.

Unless it's relevant, keep it minimal. Your pie charts only show off how much you studied for the subject at hand. Too many and you'll just overwhelm everyone with needless information. Their time is just as valuable as yours, so maintain that integrity and tell them what they need to know, not everything they don't.

Don't Assume Anything

Well, we all know how looked down upon stereotyping is. To say it's an awful thing to do would be an understatement. So, please, *don't* assume anything about your audience. Have a certain political stance? Favorite color? Are you trying to figure out if they're all rich? Don't.

Just do the opposite of Nike - *don't* do it. Assuming anything like this about your audience can make it so that your presentation becomes obsolete.

If you walk into a room and just assume that everyone is a fan of Nickelback, you're going to have a bad day. There are ways to figure out these things about your audience - starting your presentation or speech by blasting *Look at This Photograph* for the entirety of the song is probably not your best move, no matter how much you might like the song.

Ignoring Is Not Bliss

Are you passionate about your subject? If you answered yes, then this applies to you. I know that sometimes we can get swept away with our subject and go on for hours. We want everyone to know just how great it is! Like everything in life, though – there's a catch. You might forget that your audience exists. That, and they may not know the subject at hand, so it's up to you to explain it to them. Going on rants about it won't help them and they'll easily become bored.

You should always let your audience know what they're in for before you begin. This allows them to understand it better. Taking questions at the end of the presentation is also a good idea, as you can always give them the information they're looking for if you've not touched on it. You want them to be able to focus on the presentation at hand without getting lost. So, don't ignore them! Be sure to always keep them in mind as you go along while explaining things openly.

Overselling

So, you have a presentation that's more of a sales meeting. Okay, I can roll with that. Do you know what the biggest mistake is when trying to sell a product in a meeting? It's right in the title. Overselling. We all know that a salesman is either super charismatic or that dingy person in cartoons trying to sell broken products. I don't believe either of these to be true in real life - they're just stereotypes.

That being said, it can be easy for people to pick up on these kinds of first impressions because of those stereotypes. Nothing will turn a customer off more from buying or investing in your product like overselling. I know this sounds basic, but I'm sure you're wondering to yourself how not to oversell. Well, there are a few things you can do.

Use open-ended questions. For example, instead of saying, "What do you mean your company can't afford this product?" You should ask, "What kind of price would you pay for so-and-so features/abilities?" Don't try to cut your customer off by appearing disgruntled if they can't afford a product, or are questioning the amount. Try to reason with them why the amount is worth it, instead of forcing them to buy.

This goes hand in hand with empathy. Be sure to be empathetic while presenting. You want to find points where you can understand why they're interested in the product. Depending on the product, they might have a need that only your product can offer. You can always talk about personal experiences with them, and ask them questions as to why they feel their current products aren't doing the best job.

Overselling is dangerous when it comes to sales, but by being genuine in your understanding and being open to questions that your audience might have, you'll find that you'll naturally have a more charismatic presentation.

Offensive Is Not Effective

It's a new world out there. Humor is not what it was years ago, as the internet has made it, so we're changing. Our society has become more aware of edgy humor, and it's certainly not as commonplace as it was. At the same time, humor is also objective, and not everyone laughs at the same jokes. That's okay. Sometimes it's based on our own lives or how we grew up. This doesn't mean that there should be any offensive material in a presentation. Those jokes that were okay are no longer representations of language that we should use. You need to be more concerned about how your humor might affect your audience and take into account all walks of life. Crass humor is no longer appreciated - it's just offensive.

When used properly, humor is a fantastic way to immerse your audience and ensure that they laugh and enjoy themselves. There's a fine line with humor, though. There are times when it can go overboard. Some humor in presentations is an excellent tool to relax your audience, build rapport, and enhance your presentation. However, bad jokes will always be bad jokes. And someone laughing at their own bad jokes is even more uncomfortable to watch. Know your audience and always avoid jokes about politics or religion or anything sexist or racist.

Instead look for humorous stories in your own life to share, especially when the joke is on you; self-deprecating humor can be very funny and endearing. When people are relaxed, they take in information more effectively so making them smile and laugh can be very useful during your presentation; just leave out the bad jokes and controversial material.

Avoid the Ego

I believe that pride is a virtue - if you've managed to get to the point where you are now; I see no reason why you shouldn't be proud of yourself. That being said, ego and pride share a very slimline and most of it is limited when we are surrounded by others.

When you're speaking to a crowd it can be easy to get a little cocky, especially if you're a professional on your subject. You know all the latest up-to-date information because you've researched the subject for months, if not years. You may have even dedicated your life to it. So why wouldn't people need to listen to you? You have the information, and you're basically giving it away.

This view can give you an abundance of confidence, which people will appreciate. You'll need to watch your tone when you deliver the information, though. When you allow ego to take hold of your attitude and your actions, you'll end up with a crowd that no longer feels happy to be there. They'll feel like they're being lectured to. You'll lose the connection with them because they'll feel as though their opinions or thoughts don't matter. It'll seem as though your mind is occupied by your own grandeur, rather than stimulating your audience.

110

This also goes if you have a difficult person in the audience. Don't give in to their moods and don't reflect the mood back onto them. If you have someone asking you inane questions, just try to answer them the best you can until they pass. Don't allow them to prevent you from continuing your presentation. The audience will deeply respect it.

About the Presentation

There's no doubt that we have routines that we do when we're presenting. After all, it's always easier to do something we've always done rather than change it. Sometimes, though, these mistakes we're making can be debilitating to our presentation. We might not even know we're messing up at the moment! No one tells us - so we continue to make the same mistakes, all while being blissfully unaware. Don't worry if you find yourself making these common mistakes and just try to work them out as you go along. Once you know that they're present, you can then begin to rule them out.

Using Fillers

You might think that fillers are just information dumps, but it's actually based on the words you're using while presenting. So, what do I mean by fillers? Um, you know, I mean, it's really hard to say. Did you notice something about that sentence? Those are the fillers I'm referring to. They're the words we use as backups when we have nothing of note to say, or if we've forgotten a part of our presentation. Unfortunately, these words make the audience question how professional you are. Try to avoid these words when you feel them on the tip of your tongue. If you do feel them coming up, you can always

111

add a pause between your sentences to fill the momentary space - just be sure you don't pause for too long!

Is That A Question?

Have you ever heard someone speak in a way that makes it sound as though everything their saying sounds like a question? Well, this is a natural thing that can happen when we're trying to get someone's attention. It's gone about all the wrong way, though. You need to have reflection after each question, and if everything you're saying sounds like one, it gives off the wrong impression to the audience. So, keep them to a minimum and use them only for impact.

The Funny Guy

Okay, humor is great. I love humor as much as the next person, as it can help entertain your audience. There's nothing like getting everyone in the room to laugh at once - it's an amazing feeling! It can also help if you're talking about a serious subject that can cause negativity in the room. It's a wonderful tool to utilize that sets everyone at ease.

So, what's wrong with a little humor? Nothing. This applies only if you're using too much humor. You must remember that public speaking differs from being a comedian. You're not up there to crack jokes constantly as though you're at a comedy club. This is about delivering a speech or a presentation that wows the audience. You'll want to keep your humor to lighten the mood, otherwise, your audience may not take you seriously and your presentation will be wholly misremembered.

Practice, Practice, Practice

You might notice that most public speakers don't mess up. I know that in the beginning, I never truly prepared. Where did that leave me? adlibbing. No one adlibs unless they've walked into the room unprepared. To get the best results for your presentation, practice as much as you need to. Some people need to practice a dozen times, others even more. Once you practice enough that you feel comfortable, you're ready to step out on that stage. I will say, though, once you start to get better at public speaking, you'll feel the need to leave out the practicing. Don't do it! Always practice, or you might just find yourself speechless in front of a crowd that's hanging onto your every word.

Timing Is Everything

So, you've practiced. Did you make a small mistake to not check something while you were practicing? I know I did at the beginning of my career. There's a trick to public speaking that is integral to your engagement - the time! Time yourself during every practice. You shouldn't be halfway through the allotted time and only have two more slides to go. You should be prepared and fill in the time (if you have any extra while practicing) with information that the audience should know, not just fillers that will leave them bored.

If you know that there will be audience participation, then leave some time for that. Give yourself about a third of your presentation to questions, should they be something the presentation needs. Otherwise, leave only a few minutes towards the end for audience participation and leave it at that. Then, once all the questions have been asked, use your closing line. You want to make sure that you don't walk off the stage as soon as the last person asks the question. Always have a closing line available to let everyone in the room know that you've finished. You don't want them wasting their time seeing if you'll come back.

Houston, We Have Technical Issues

We've all been there. One minute you're getting set up for your presentation, but when you turn to look at your slideshow, the projector isn't working and the screen is black. Technical difficulties are frustrating and make it awkward for starting a presentation. You can't always stop technical issues from showing up, as it might not be your fault – could be the venue, the internet connection, or even the lighting. Some things will be out of your hands. There are ways that you can avoid some of these issues, though.

If you've never presented at the location before, show up early so that you can set everything up. If you can't show up early, be sure to ask some questions about previous speakers and any technical issues they've encountered before. This way you can look up these issues and be well-versed in fixing them if you can. You can always practice with connecting your computer to different outputs and displays or bring a friend along who knows computers well.

As long as you take charge when these situations do happen, instead of standing there dumbfounded, you won't lose your appeal to the audience. Yes, it'll be frustrating. Yes, you can't always control it, but you can control how you react and what you do in the time that you're waiting for the situation to be fixed.

114

Liar, Liar

I understand that, if you have something that you desperately need to sell, you might become desperate. You don't want to do this transgression because, if you get figured out, you'll not only lose your audience, but you might lose a whole lot more. You never, ever want to lie about your facts. Always use proper sources.

Don't up the numbers of your sales and don't fabricate important details. These changes, which might seem minute to you, might be a big red flag to someone who really knows the subject at hand. It doesn't matter if you're standing in front of your class or a client, you need to have your facts straight. You should already know the information off the top of your head, and where you got the information. Wikipedia isn't always the resource you think it is.

Prepare yourself in case people do question your research or your numbers. Tell them exactly where they came from. This will be easy if you've prepared properly. So, don't lie. The only one you'll be lying to in the end is you, and it'll only make you feel uneasy when the presentation's finished.

Let Go of Mistakes

There will be times when you can't control what happens - whether it's a technological error (which happens more often than we'd like) or a missing slide during a presentation that you hadn't noticed. It's harsh to say, but there's a high chance that you'll make mistakes regardless of how careful you are. You need to anticipate them because they'll happen more often than not. It's all about constant improvement and learning from your mistakes.

No matter what, you'll grow from your mistakes, just as I did in my early career. To reach your goals you'll always need to plan ahead. The mistakes you make do not define who you are because mistakes are inevitable, and all you can do is prepare yourself for those mistakes the next time around. You'll have to be able to let that go and learn how to do better the next time.

They don't automatically make you any less of a great public speaker - even if it's the kind of mistake that you end up being upset afterward. If anything, they're an opportunity to grow and adapt to your work. So, don't make the mistake of believing that you're a failure just because you messed up. Brush it off, learn from it, and take another step forward - that's the secret to growth and success.

Overcoming Fear - Profile - You

I want you to envision yourself standing in front of a crowd of hundreds. You walk out on stage, and the crowd applauds as you step out and stand in front of them. You smile at the audience. The light is blinding from where you're standing, and you can barely make out the faces of everyone in the audience. Despite this, you can tell that the theatre is full.

You can feel your heart racing in your chest, but you accept it and bring the microphone to your mouth. You breathe out slowly before you

116

introduce yourself. There are no mistakes and there are no fumbles. It's just you and the audience, and they're hanging onto every word.

This is your story and I know you can make it happen. I want you to visualize whatever it is you see yourself doing and practice it as you go. Write down your goals, celebrate your accomplishments, and revel in the fact that you're making a difference in not only your life but in the lives of others.

Now you just have to put in the work.

FINAL WORDS

Public speaking is a life-changing career, as it teaches you discipline, confidence, and pride. It can be a platform to share your ideas and move others to act on what you believe to be important. When I tell people how my life changed once I began public speaking, many didn't believe me. It was through hard work and years of learning that I was able to show how my life has changed. There are days when even I look around in awe. I've been fortunate enough to have seen this same transformation in so many people - from CEOs to philanthropists.

I know that the concepts in this book will lead you down a path that, at this moment in time, might be difficult to fathom. You'll find yourself performing better at work with each meeting or that you're no longer scared to shake that man at the pub's hand. Maybe you're no longer nervous to give that toast at your best friend's wedding. Whatever the case may be, I know that you can overcome it so long as you follow the principles I've laid out for you.

Being a part of your breakthrough gives me the motivation to continue speaking and helping others. I can only hope that you'll grow to accomplish incredible things, and I'm so grateful to you for allowing me to play a part in that. I've only set up the ways you can do this but you'll have to set it in motion.

This is the part where you take the reins and get to work. I recommend re-reading whichever part speaks most to you, and use this book to your advantage as you excel in your own public speaking career. All it takes is one step and your journey has just begun.

REFERENCES

"7 Things You Need to Know About Fear." Psychology Today, Sussex Publishers, www.psychologytoday.com/us/blog/smashing-the-brainblocks/201511/7-things-you-need-know-about-fear.

"Acknowledging Your Fear and Finding Your Way Forward -." The Center for Transformational Presence, 12 Feb. 2019, www.transformationalpresence.org/alan-seale-blog/acknowledging-your-fear-and-finding-your-way-forward/

Beqiri, Gini. "Best Practices for Designing Presentation Slides." VirtualSpeech, VirtualSpeech, 20 Sept. 2018, www.virtualspeech.com/blog/designing-presentation-slides.

Boundless. "Boundless Communications." Lumen, www.courses.lumenlearning.com/boundless-communications/chapter/steps-of-preparing-a-speech/.

Chapter 5: Adapting to Your Audience, www.cengage.com/resource_uploads/static_resources/0534637272/16296/PSEA_Summary_c05_rc.htm.

"Chris Guillebeau." It's Not About Overcoming Your Fears; It's About Acknowledging and Moving On : The Art of Non-Conformity, www.chrisguillebeau.com/acknowledging-and-moving-on/

"Fear." Psychology Today, Sussex Publishers, www.psychologytoday.com/us/basics/fear.

"Fear of Public Speaking: How Can I Overcome It?" Mayo Clinic, Mayo Foundation for Medical Education and Research, 17 May 2017, www.mayoclinic.org/diseases-conditions/specific-phobias/expert-answers/fear-ofpublic-speaking/faq-20058416.

Fearn, Nicholas. "Best Presentation Software of 2020: Slides for Speeches and Talks." TechRadar, TechRadar Pro, www.techradar.com/best/best-presentation-software.

Grayson, Lee. "Setting the Tone of a Speech." Small Business - Chron.com, Chron.com, 21 Nov. 2017, www.smallbusiness.chron.com/setting-tone-speech-41439.html.

Hart, Bridgett. "4 Strategies to Overcome Fear Paralysis." Medium, Medium, 29 Oct. 2013, www.medium.com/@hartconnections/4-strategies-to-overcome-fear-paralysis-93effc462dd.

Hoque, Faisal. "7 Methods to Overcome Your Fear of Failure." Fast Company, Fast Company, 10 June 2015, www.fastcompany.com/3046944/7-methods-to-overcome-your-fear-of-failure.

How to use humor effectively in speeches. (2016). https://www.write-out-loud.com/how-to-use-humor-effectively.html

"How to Design a Presentation." Lucidpress, 10 Sept. 2018, www.lucidpress.com/pages/learn/how-to-design-presentations.

Humphrey, Judith. "You Are Probably Making One of These 7 Mistakes in Your Everyday Speech." Fast Company, Fast Company, 7 Mar. 2019, www.fastcompany.com/90314736/you-are-probably-making-one-of-these-7-mistakes-in-your-everyday-speech.

Layton, Julia. "How Fear Works." HowStuffWorks Science, HowStuffWorks, 26 July 2019, www.science.howstuffworks.com/life/inside-the-mind/emotions/fear7.htm.

Lott, Tim. "Children Used to Be Scared of the Dark – Now They Fear Failure." The Guardian, Guardian News and Media, 29 May 2015, www.theguardian.com/lifeandstyle/2015/may/29/children-used-to-be-scared-of-the-dark-now-they-fear-failure.

Morgan, Nick. "How to Become an Authentic Speaker." Harvard Business Review, 2 Jan. 2019, www.hbr.org/2008/11/how-to-become-an-authentic-speaker.

Nediger, Midori, and Midori. "Presentation Design Guide: How to Summarize Information for Presentations." Venngage, 12 Nov. 2019, www.venngage.com/blog/presentation-design/.

Palmer, Belinda. "Fear Paralysis Reflex, Anxiety, and Panic Attacks." Friends and Family Health Centers Blog, www.homewoodfriendsandfamily.com/blog/2019/10/15/fear-paralysis-reflex-anxiety-and-panic-attacks/.

Parashar, Avish. "How to Add Humor to Your Speech-without Being a Comedian." Ragan Communications, 10 Aug. 2018, www.ragan.com/how-to-add-humor-to-your-speech-without-being-a-comedian-2/.

Ronnie Higgins. "Fun Activities to Spice Up Your Next Workshop (9 Ideas): Eventbrite." Eventbrite US Blog, 2 Dec. 2019, www.eventbrite.com/blog/9-ideas-to-spice-up-your-workshop-or-training-and-engage-your-audience-ds00/.

Ropeik, David. "The Consequences of Fear." EMBO Reports, U.S. National Library of Medicine, Oct. 2004, www.ncbi.nlm.nih.gov/pmc/articles/PMC1299209/.

Saab, A. T. J. A. L. C. (2017, October 27). What Happens in the Brain When We Feel Fear. https://www.smithsonianmag.com/science-nature/what-happens-brain-feel-fear-180966992/

Schmitt, Jeff. "10 Keys to Writing A Speech." Forbes, Forbes Magazine, 5 Feb. 2016, www.forbes.com/sites/jeffschmitt/2013/07/16/10-keys-to-writing-a-speech/#60cad69d4fb7.

"Single Post." Commanding presence, www.commandingpresence.com/single-post/2019/06/10/4-Tips-for-a-Commanding-Presence

Smith, Jacquelyn. "12 Tips for Overcoming Your Fear of Change at Work." Forbes, Forbes Magazine, 17 Jan. 2014, www.forbes.com/sites/jacquelynsmith/2014/01/17/12-tips-for-overcoming-your-fear-of-change-at-work-2/#10ec8c102735

Smith, Jacquelyn. "13 Public Speaking Mistakes You Don't Want to Make." Business Insider, Business Insider, 4 Feb. 2016, www.businessinsider.com/avoid-these-public-speaking-mistakes-2016-2#-13.

"Transitions in a Speech or Presentation." Manner of Speaking, 12 May 2019, www.mannerofspeaking.org/2019/05/12/transitions-in-a-speech-or-presentation/

van Mulukom, V. (2018, December 10). How imagination can help people overcome fear and anxiety. http://theconversation.com/how-imagination-can-help-people-overcome-fear-and-anxiety-108209

"Westside Toastmasters Is Located in Los Angeles and Santa Monica, California." Inspire Your Audience - Chapter 3: Preparation: The Source of a Speaker's Power,

www.westsidetoastmasters.com/resources/powerspeak/ch03.html.

YOUR FREE GIFT IS HERE!

Thank you for purchasing this book. As a token and supplement to your new learnings and personal development journey, you will receive this booklet as a gift, and it's completely free.

This includes - as already announced in this book - a valuable resource of simple approach and actionable ideas to mastermind your own routine towards a more calm and confident way to tackle your everyday.

This booklet will provide you a powerful insight on:

- How to formulate empowering habits that can change your life
- Masterminding your own Power of 3
- Just the 3 things you need to drastically change your life and how you feel about yourself
- How to boost your self-esteem and self-awareness
- Creating a positive feedback loop everyday

You can get the bonus booklet as follows:

To access the secret download page, open a browser window on your computer or smartphone and enter: bonus.gerardshaw.com

You will be automatically directed to the download page.

Please note that this bonus booklet may be available for download for a limited time only.

Printed in Great Britain
by Amazon

78708048R00078